LifeLight

*"In Him was life, and the life was the light of men."* John 1:4

# Creation, New Creation

## LEADERS GUIDE

CONCORDIA PUBLISHING HOUSE • SAINT LOUIS

From the study:

God's highest creation on the earth is man and woman. They are created for fellowship with God. As God's representatives over creation, they are to cultivate the earth's resources and, with the attitude of mutual respect, care and provide for those different than themselves. Moreover, man and woman, as husband and wife, are to be faithful and of mutual service to each other as they reflect the love of God, who in Jesus Christ is shown to be self-giving. Through constant dependence upon the God of creative love and constant fellowship with Him through Jesus Christ, each person's life reaches its fullest meaning.

3558 S. Jefferson Ave., St. Louis, MO 63118-3968
1-800-325-3040 • www.cph.org



Written by Richard Joseph Shuta

Edited by Brian Chisamore

Field testing coordinated by Rev. Eric Van Scyoc, St. Thomas Lutheran Church, Rocky River, OH.

Cover illustration by Sally Wern Comport © Concordia Publishing House



This publication may be available in Braille, in large print, or on cassette tape for the visually impaired. Please allow 8 to 12 weeks for delivery. Write to Lutheran Blind Mission, 7550 Watson Rd., St. Louis, MO 63119-4409; call toll-free 1-888-215-2455; or visit the Web site: www.blindmission.org.

Manufactured in the United States of America

1 2 3 4 5 6 7 8 9 10   19 18 17 16 15 14 13 12 11 10

# Contents

# Introduction

## Welcome to LifeLight

A special pleasure is in store for you. You will be instrumental in leading your brothers and sisters in Christ closer to Him who is our life and light (John 1:4). You will have the pleasure of seeing fellow Christians discover new insights and rediscover old ones as they open the Scriptures and dig deep into them, perhaps deeper than they have ever dug before. More than that, you will have the pleasure of sharing in this wonderful study.

## LifeLight—An In-depth Study

LifeLight is a series of in-depth Bible studies. The goal of LifeLight is that through a regular program of in-depth personal and group study of Scripture, more and more Christian adults may grow in their personal faith in Jesus Christ, enjoy fellowship with the members of His body, and reach out in love to others in witness and service.

*In-depth* means that this Bible study includes the following four components: individual daily home study; discussion in a small group; a lecture presentation on the Scripture portion under study; and an enhancement of the week's material (through reading the enrichment magazine).

## LifeLight Participants

LifeLight participants are adults who desire a deeper study of the Scriptures than is available in the typical Sunday morning adult Bible class. (Mid-to-older teens might also be LifeLight participants.) While LifeLight does not assume an existing knowledge of the Bible or special experience or skills in Bible study, it does assume a level of commitment that will bring participants to each of the nine weekly assemblies having read the assigned readings and attempted to answer the study questions. Daily reading and study will require from 15 to 30 minutes for the five days preceding the LifeLight assembly. The day following the assembly will be spent reviewing the previous week's study by going over the completed study leaflet and the enrichment magazine.

## LifeLight Leadership

While the in-depth process used by LifeLight begins with individual study and cannot achieve its aims without this individual effort, it cannot be completed by individual study alone. Therefore, trained leaders are necessary. You fill one or perhaps more of the important roles described below.

### The Director

This person oversees the LifeLight program in a local center (which may be a congregation or a center operated by several neighboring congregations). The director

- serves as the parish LifeLight overall coordinator and leader;
- coordinates the scheduling of the LifeLight program;
- orders materials;
- convenes LifeLight leadership-team meetings;
- develops publicity materials;
- recruits participants;
- maintains records and budgeting;
- assigns, with the leadership-team, participants to small discussion groups;
- makes arrangements for facilities;
- communicates outreach opportunities to small-group leaders and to congregational boards;
- follows up on participants who leave the program.

### The Assistant Director *(optional)*

This person may assist the director. Duties listed for the director may be assigned to the assistant director as mutually agreeable.

### The Lecture Leader

This person prepares and delivers the lecture at the weekly assembly. (Lesson material for the lecture leader begins on p. 8.) The lecture leader

- prepares and presents the Bible study lecture to the large group;

- prepares worship activities (devotional thought, hymn, prayer), using resources in the study leaflet and leaders guide and possibly other, outside sources;
- helps the small-group discussion leaders to grow in understanding the content of the lessons;
- encourages prayer at weekly leadership-team and discussion-leaders meetings.

### The Small-Group Coordinator *(optional; the director may fill this role)*

This person supervises and coordinates the work of the small-group discussion leaders. The small-group coordinator

- recruits with the leadership-team the small-group discussion leaders;
- trains or arranges for training of the discussion leaders;
- assists the director and discussion leaders in follow-up and outreach;
- encourages the discussion leaders to contact absent group members;
- participates in the weekly leadership-team and discussion-leaders equipping meetings;
- provides ongoing training and support as needed.

### The Small-Group Discussion Leaders

These people guide and facilitate discussion of LifeLight participants in the small groups. (Lesson material for the small-group leaders begins on p. 53.) There should be one discussion leader for every group of no more than twelve participants. The small-group discussion leaders are, perhaps, those individuals who are most important to the success of the program. They should, therefore, be chosen with special care and be equipped with skills needed to guide discussion and to foster a caring fellowship within the group. These discussion leaders

- prepare each week for the small-group discussion by using the study leaflet and small-group leaders guide section for that session **(see p. 57)**;
- read the enrichment magazine as a study supplement;
- guide and facilitate discussion in their small group;
- encourage and assist the discussion group in prayer;
- foster fellowship and mutual care within the discussion group;
- attend weekly discussion leaders training meetings.

## Leadership Training

LifeLight leaders will meet weekly to review the previous week's work and plan the coming week. At this session, leaders can address concerns and prepare for the coming session. LifeLight is a 1½-hour program with no possibility for it to be taught in the one hour typically available on Sunday mornings. Some congregations, however, may want to use the Sunday morning Bible study hour for LifeLight preparation and leadership training. In such a meeting, the lecture leader and/or small-group coordinator may lead the discussion leaders through the coming week's lesson, reserving 5 or 10 minutes for problem solving or other group concerns.

While it requires intense effort, LifeLight has proven to bring great benefit to LifeLight participants. The effort put into this program, both by leaders and by participants, will be rewarding and profitable.

## The LifeLight Weekly Schedule

Here is how LifeLight will work week by week:

1. Before session 1, each participant will receive the study leaflet for session 1 and the enrichment magazine for the course. The study leaflet contains worship resources (for use both in individual daily study and at the opening of the following week's assembly) and readings and study questions for five days. Challenge questions will lead those participants who have the time and desire a greater challenge into even deeper levels of study.

2. After the five days of individual study at home, participants will gather for a weekly assembly of all LifeLight participants. The assembly will begin with a brief period of worship (5 minutes). Participants will then join their assigned small discussion groups (of twelve or fewer, who will remain the same throughout the course), where they will go over the week's study questions together (55 minutes). Assembling together once again, participants will listen to a lecture presentation on the readings they have studied in the previous week and discussed in their small groups (20 minutes). After the lecture presentation, the director or another leader will distribute the study leaflet for the following week. Closing announcements and other necessary business

may take another five minutes before dismissal.

In some places some small groups will not join the weekly assembly because of scheduling or other reasons. Such groups may meet at another time and place (perhaps in the home of one of the small group's members). Those congregations may record the lecture given by the lecture leader at the weekly assembly and duplicate it for use by other groups meeting later in the week.

3. On the day following the assembly, participants will review the preceding week's work by rereading the study leaflet they completed (and that they perhaps supplemented or corrected during the discussion in their small group) and by reading appropriate articles in the enrichment magazine.

Then the LifeLight weekly study process will begin all over again!

## Recommended Study Resources and Worship

*The Lutheran Study Bible.* St. Louis: Concordia Publishing House, 2009. This resource contains more than 26,000 study and application notes, a most thorough reference guide (pp. lxv–cx), and over 90,000 cross-references, as well as a 31,000-entry concordance, maps, charts, and timelines.

*Concordia Self-Study Bible, New International Version.* St. Louis: Concordia Publishing House, 1986. Interpretive notes on each page form a running commentary on the text. The book includes cross-references, a 35,000-word concordance, full-color maps, charts, and timelines.

Roehrs, Walter R., and Martin H. Franzmann. *Concordia Self-Study Commentary.* St. Louis: Concordia Publishing House, 1979. This one-volume commentary on the Bible contains 950 pages and is tailored for lay use.

*The Concordia Organist* is a 31-CD collection of pipe organ accompaniments for all the hymns and liturgical music in *Lutheran Service Book*. St. Louis: Concordia Publishing House (order no. 99-2264). Use these CDs for worship hymn accompaniment.

*Every Voice a Song* Pipe Organ Accompaniment for 180 Hymns and Liturgy. St. Louis: Concordia Publishing House (order no. 99-1565). Use this music CD for worship hymn accompaniment.

# The God of Creation

## Genesis 1:1–25; Acts 14:8–17

*Preparing for the Session*

## Central Focus

The universe and all that is in it is the result of the creative act of the triune God. The universe is not of the same essence of God, nor is anything in the universe to be given the fear, love, and trust that belongs only to God. The power, wisdom, goodness, and generosity of God seen in creation is meant to lead us to seek out the Creator so that we enter into a right relationship with the one God, who is the source of all existence.

## Objectives

That participants, led by the Holy Spirit working through God's Word, will

1. recognize that creation comes from the hand of a wise and generous Creator;

2. be alert to the temptation of fearing, loving, and trusting in things more than in God, their giver; and

3. share the good news that the greatest gift to creation is the triune God's redemption of it through the Son of God, who brings freedom from slavery to man-made idols, which cannot fulfill human need.

**Note for small-group leaders:** Lesson notes and other materials you will need begin on page 57.

## For the Lecture Leader

*Session Plan*

### Worship

Begin the session with the hymn printed in the study leaflet. Accompaniments are available in denominational hymnals, such as *Lutheran Service Book* or *Lutheran Worship* (refer to hymnal index). (Note: Concordia Publishing House has available *The Concordia Organist*. All the initial worship hymns in the LifeLight courses are included in this resource. It's especially helpful for mission congregations and small parishes. See the list of study resources on page 7.) Follow with this prayer:

### Prayer

O divine Creator, Father, Son, and Holy Spirit, grant us the ability to listen to Your revelation in the Scriptures so that we might see Your goodness, generosity, and power all around us in Creation. Guard us against the idolatry of fearing, loving, or trusting in any part of creation rather than in You. May we offer to You alone the trust, obedience, gratitude, and honor due Your name because of Your multiple gifts in creation to us. We thank You especially for the fullness of life and the light to the way of salvation given in Jesus Christ. Amen.

## Lecture Presentation

### Introduction

Visitors to the Grand Canyon are told that the magnificent vista is the result of a slow dripping of water from the Colorado River over millions of years. A Christian visitor looking upon that same vista will see much more. He will recognize the living God's handiwork behind the "dripping" of the water. Such an origin of the canyon—indeed, the origin of the entire universe—is known only by "special revelation," which is given by the Creator Himself and recorded in the inspired Scriptures.

Despite all the probing of science, the origin of creation remains a mystery. Scripture comments, (Ecclesiastes 11:5) "As you do not know the way the spirit comes to the bones in the womb of a woman with child, so you do not know the work of God who makes everything" (see also Job 38:4–41). Knowledge of why there is a creation and who it is who brought creation into existence lies outside the analysis of modern science.

Scripture does not explain scientifically how God created the world. Unlike scientists, who have the God-given right to examine such things as *how* things presently are, the ancient biblical writers concentrated on *who* gave creation its existence and for what purpose creation exists. Therefore, the Bible presents creation in a nonscientific way. Of course, that is not the same thing as saying that the biblical texts are unscientific. Both Jesus Christ and the apostle Paul accepted the Genesis account of creation as historically accurate. When Jesus speaks of the creation of male and female and the institution of marriage in the Garden of Eden (Matthew 19:4–5), He quotes Genesis 1:27 and 2:24. Likewise, the apostle Paul, according to 2 Corinthians 4:6, refers to God's creation of light. In Romans 5:12–21, Paul describes the significance of Jesus' ministry as His ability to undo the havoc Adam brought down upon creation.

## 1 Creation Exists Because There Is One Creator (Genesis 1:1–2)

The Book of Genesis opens with the simple yet majestic and profound declaration, (1:1) "In the beginning, God created the heavens and the earth." "The heavens and the earth" refers to the universe. St. Augustine, a great fifth-century Church leader, pointed out that God did not create "in time," but with God's act of creation, time and space came into existence. Scripture does not specify when the universe, including the earth, was brought into existence. Scripture's record of *human* history on earth goes back only several thousand years.

Because only God is eternal, the great "I AM" (Exodus 3:14), and source and sustainer of all that presently exists (Acts 17:28), only He could create the universe out of nothing but His Word (Hebrews 11:3). There were no preexistent substances, nothing to hinder His power. In a moment when there was nothing, all things both visible and invisible came into existence through a free act of the personal Creator.

In a theological sense, only God creates, brings into existence from nothing. Human builders and artisans simply rearrange materials already in existence. Moses, Jesus, and St. Paul affirm that there is only one Creator, God, who is the source of all reality (Deuteronomy 6:4; Mark 12:29). The Hebrew word used for "create" (*bara'*) is never used with a subject other than *God* in the Old Testament.

The prophet Isaiah records this warning from God to people of various cultures, with their so-called competing deities: (Isaiah 44:24) "Thus says the LORD, your Redeemer, who formed you from the womb: I am the LORD, who made all things, who alone stretched out the heavens, who spread out the earth by Myself."

Some people may be surprised to learn that Genesis does not attempt to prove God's existence. Hebrews 3:4 takes it as a logical conclusion that the existence of the universe points to a Creator when it says, "Every house is built by someone, but the builder of all things is God." Scripture declares that a person is a "fool," acting irrationally, who says there is no God (Psalm 14:1). Romans 1:19–21 testifies that God has surrounded all people with the evidence of a Creator simply by being surrounded by creation's grandeur, complexity, and power. Additionally, the internal testimony of each person's conscience, which is our built-in sense of "oughtness" ("I ought to do this" or "I ought to avoid that") (Romans 2:14–15), should lead them to seek to learn more about who or what gives everything its value (Acts 17:27) and who eventually judges all actions.

Nevertheless, atheists (from the Greek *a*, "not," and *theos*, "god") strongly deny the existence of any Supreme Being. Some atheists argue that religion is a psychological crutch that emotionally weak persons use to get through life. Certainly, those who believe in God's existence acknowledge that the belief fulfills their emotional need. But the atheists' argument can be turned against them. It can be said that atheists find the existence of God threatening. Therefore, their rejection of a God to whom they are accountable is an emotionally comfortable crutch, a psychic pathology, and even worse, a willful suppression of the truth of God's existence that will condemn them (Romans 1:18).

Scripture reveals that the universe was created by God the Father (1 Corinthians 8:6), through the Son (John 1:10; Colossians 1:16), and in the Holy Spirit (Genesis 1:2).

## 2 Genesis's Description of God and Creation (Genesis 1:3–25)

At the very beginning of God's seven creation days, the earth was unorganized, "without form and void" (Genesis 1:2). But then the Spirit of God began "hovering" over the face of the waters. Later rabbis would say that such action of the Spirit was like that of the dove. Many years later, the Holy Spirit objectively confirmed His presence at the Son of God's Baptism by the appearance of a dove (Matthew 3:16).

Verse 3—God spoke light into existence. Light was present before the creation of the light-bearing bodies, the sun and stars. Genesis 1 does not use the terms "sun" and "moon" because they were associated with the names of pagan deities. The Genesis narrative clearly maintains that the planets are only planets, and not gods. This opened the way for science in the Western world, since it no longer needs to fear investigating the planets. It also helps followers of Scripture to avoid seeking guidance of day-to-day activities through astrology.

Verses 4–5—With the light came the evening-morning cycle. The earth began its rotation on its axis. This ended God's creative activity on the first day.

Verses 6–8—These verses do not focus on the cosmos (ordered universe) generally, but on planet Earth specifically. They present Creation Day 2. That is the day when the earth's atmosphere came into existence. God parted the waters below the earth from those above. These two sets of water were separated from one another by the expanse (firmament) of the earth's atmosphere. The "Heaven," mentioned in verse 8 refers collectively to the sky and space.

Verses 9–13—Now we come to Creation Day 3, when the continents, oceans, and land vegetation appeared. God gave the vegetation the mechanisms for self-reproduction (the meaning of "kind"; v. 11). This mechanism was one of the instruments of God's continuing involvement in creation, His Divine Providence (discussed in Lesson 4).

On Creation Day 3, God caused the earth to rise out of the waters to be inhabitable by man (Job 38:10–11). Afterward, it brought forth plants at God's command. Plants are more closely related to the earth than are either animals or humans. Plants take root in the earth, from which minerals are taken for their construction.

Verses 14–19—On Creation Day 4, the light-bearing bodies were "turned on." The words describing the fourth day emphasize the light more than the sun and stars. The night-day cycle set in motion on Day 1, however, continued without interruption.

Verses 20–23—On Creation Day 5, fish and birds were created. Genesis emphasizes the huge quantities of water-living creatures that God created. Among these water-living creatures were (v. 21) "sea creatures," literally, "long, stretched beings." Various types of winged birds were also created. These creatures also were blessed with mechanisms for reproduction (v. 22).

Verses 24–25—On Creation Day 6, God first created land animals. God's activity was more pronounced in their creation. There is variety in the animal world. Verse 24 categorizes them as either cattle (all animals that can be domesticated), creepers (smaller land animals such as worms, insects, and rabbits), or beasts (animals not easily or casually tamed, such as lions). The land animals did not receive a blessing from God, as did the water animals, the fowl, and (later) man. Perhaps if the land animals multiplied without restraint, this would be unhealthy to human existence. However, both the birds and the land animals were authorized to eat from every green plant on the earth (Genesis 1:30). Because sin had not yet entered into life on earth, the animal, fish, and insect world were no threat to human existence.

Thus, God methodically and progressively established the universe. God is a God of order and purpose (1 Corinthians 14:40). When God saw His creations, He called them "good" (Genesis 1:25; see also 1 Timothy 4:4). Science today owes much to the nature of God the Creator. Science affirms the reality of the physical world and science assumes that nature possesses a traceable, understandable order. From that original goodness of creation, the applied sciences take their origin.

## 3 Creation Is Distinct from and Dependent upon the Creator

Some contemporary people in the Western world are now flirting with ideas that have their origin in ancient Eastern religions. These religions teach that all that exists is simply an unfolding of an impersonal world force. Philosophically, this "may the force be with you!" belief is called *Monism*. According to Monism, "God" is neither a "he," a "she," nor anything "objective" or "personal." No personal supreme Creator exists. Monism's position is that the universe is closed to any intervention from an outside power. "Mother Nature" is the only so-called god to focus upon. "Salvation" is knowledge and the feeling of oneness with the impersonal "spirit" of the universe. Monism finds formal religious expression in Hinduism, Taoism, and "New Age" guru-led movements, which believe in one supreme all-encompassing impersonal being.

But Scripture is clear that the universe is not an emanation of God or His essence. As the Self-Existent One, God is the "Most High God," meaning that God is separate from and independent of everything that has been created (Psalm 113:4–6). The Creator is not bound by any of the universe's limitations. Nature minus God equals nothing. God, however, does have status independent of nature. God alone is eternal, without beginning or end (Isaiah 57:15; Malachi 3:6). Nature is simply nature and not deity.

Because God transcends all that He has created, we must be warned that God cannot be manipulated or "boxed" in by science and its assumptions, nor by the limited vision of those who worship at the altar of the latest technological products. The Genesis 11 story of the tower of Babel is a warning to all societies that think their ability to construct things to reach the "heavens" makes the seeking of and serving God's will obsolete. Towers of human pride and covetousness will crumble under divine judgment. Regardless how inventive or powerful a person and culture become, they are not God (Isaiah 31:3; Ezekiel 28:2). Material things given by God are important to human survival, but material things cannot nourish the human spirit meant to spend an eternity with God (Luke 12:15).

Christians appreciate technological advances both in medicine and in inventions that make daily activities less drudgery. But there is more to reality than what machines can create. According to 1 Timothy 4:4, everything God created is good. However, 1 Timothy goes on to say (v. 5) that turning to God in prayer and thanksgiving are necessary to the right use of the Creator's gifts. Scientific advances must be undertaken in light of God's will that they benefit all humanity.

Those people who have come to trust in the God of Scripture find confidence and comfort in knowing that God is capable of accomplishing deeds of rescue that would be impossible for any mere human being or any so-called "law of nature" to perform (Luke 1:37). To Him alone goes all glory, for He alone is Creation's lifesource and its redemption from sin's bondage (Revelation 4:11).

## 4 Looking beyond Creation to the Creator (Acts 14:8–17)

As a great missionary and master communicator, St. Paul knew how to meet the needs of his various audiences. This was evident when Paul visited Lystra, a Roman settlement in the province of Galatia with ethnically distinct people who spoke their own language.

Verses 8–11—One day when Lystra was crowded, either because the harvest was completed or it was a festival day, Paul healed a man crippled from birth. Paul's preaching also produced faith in the man's heart. But the pagan crowd, who were also listening to Paul, became emotionally charged from witnessing the healing power flowing from Paul's preaching. The crowd began to jabber in their local dialect that "the gods have come down to us in the likeness of men!"

Verses 12–13—The crowd began to address Barnabas as Zeus, the chief of the Greek family of gods. The excited crowd also thought Paul was Hermes, the Greek god of oratory, "because he [Paul] was the chief speaker." Someone must have sent word to the local priest of Zeus to begin elaborate preparations to welcome these thought-to-be-divine visitors. Because the arrangements were being made in a language unknown to Paul and Barnabas, they did not know about the blasphemous honor—the sacrifice of an animal at the town gate—that was about to be done in their honor.

Verse 14—When Barnabas and Paul realized what was about to be offered to them, the two missionaries were horrified. They did not want to be the center of such a display of idolatry that failed to distinguish the difference between God and things merely mortal. As a sign of their extreme distress over such blasphemous idolatry, the missionaries tore their garments—a typical response of protest by pious Jews. They also rushed into the crowd to stop the offering of the sacrifice.

Verse 15a—Paul asked his pagan audience why they were doing these things for them, who were mere mortals. He told them that he was simply a messenger of the good tidings that God offers to all who turn "from these vain things," to the "living God." Scripture points out that the "gods" of non-Christian religions are actually nonexistent (1 Corinthians 8:4). The followers of such religions unknowingly are serving deceiving demons rather than the good, gracious, giving God of life (1 Corinthians 10:20).

Verses 15b–17—Paul speaks about God as Creator, "who made the heaven and the earth and the sea and all that is in them." Believing in the existence of God as the Creator is essential to true faith (Hebrews 11:1, 6). Any belief that thinks humans evolved purely by chance strikes at the very foundation of the "creatorship" of God and is a futile attempt to rob God the Creator of the honor due Him, for He is the rightful creator-owner who is active in all things involving our survival. He is the God of generosity who provides the human race with vast resources of stimulating sunshine, productive soil, and life-giving rain. These blessings make the earth bountiful. Therefore, Psalm 147:8 speaks of them as a special sign of divine favor.

God's goodness in directing the seasons and elements to produce the earth's fruit to fulfill our physical needs should cause us to pause and contemplate the Giver of such goodness (Joel 2:23).

## 5 To the One God of Creation Are Fear, Love, and Trust Due

Every person has a "god" of one kind or another that

he or she is worshiping. No one is really godless, in a certain sense. We read in Psalm 31:14, "But I trust in You, O Lord; I say, 'You are my God.'" Whatever a person ultimately puts his or her fear, love, and trust in, that has become that person's god. Luther wrote of this in his explanation of the First Commandment in his Large Catechism (I 2–3):

> A god means that from which we are to expect all good and in which we are to take refuge in all distress. So, to have a God is nothing other than trusting and believing Him with the heart. . . . The confidence and faith of the heart alone make both God and an idol. If your faith and trust is right, then your god is also true.

In their quest for happiness or security, people follow competing "gods." There are the educational gods: progress, relativism, and scientism. There are the national gods: security, world power, and materialism. These gods are, however, idols, that is, "no-nothings"; they are not fundamental reality. They will let humans down. They are too small for humanity's great questions and universal needs. At times, the children of earth may get a passing thought that maybe their inventions, such as the unleashing of atoms in nuclear bombs, cannot compare to the power of Creation, as when a volcano erupts or a tsunami's waves swamp land masses. In such moments, they see that human inventions are like matches that appear bright in a dark room but are barely seen in the light of the blazing sun.

People of the earth need to hear this message from God the Creator. He says, (Isaiah 40:25–26) "To whom then will you compare Me, that I should be like him? . . . Lift up your eyes on high and see: who created these? He who brings out their host [stars] by number, calling them all by name, by the greatness of His might, and because He is strong in power not one is missing."

God is angry at sin. He says, (Exodus 20:5–6) "You shall not bow down to them [any material thing we 'idolize'] or serve them, for I the Lord your God am a jealous God." God's jealousy is His zeal to protect from destruction what He has created. For this reason, God has a firm displeasure with wickedness, especially against those who worship that which is not the only living God who is worthy to worship (Psalm 78:58).

Isaiah writes (40:21–22) that God "sits above the circle of the earth" and sees the rulers of the earth to be like mere "grasshoppers" that He can easily blow away. To God's people, the Psalmist has these comforting words: (33:18–19) "Behold, the eye of the Lord is on those who fear Him, on those who hope in His steadfast love, that He may deliver their soul from death and keep them alive in famine."

### Conclusion

Creation is essentially good because it comes from the hand of the Creator, who is good. Moreover, creation is so important to the triune God that, at a certain point in history, the Son of God personally acted within creation to redeem it and its fallen people.

God as the caring Creator is seen in the Son of God become fully man, Jesus Christ. At His Baptism, He identified with the ungodly to fulfill their righteousness (Matthew 3:13–15). He then paid for that identification with His outpoured blood upon Golgotha's Good Friday Cross (Romans 5:6). At that unique event, divine wrath, faithfulness, love, and mercy "kiss," to the benefit of all creation (Psalm 85:4, 10, 11)—and creation itself responded (Matthew 27:45, 51).

## Concluding Activities

Pray aloud: Blessed are You, O God, King of Creation; blessed are You! We thank You for Your generosity in the magnitude of Your earthly gifts to us through creation. Forgive us for those times we have been guilty of subtle idolatry, when we have forgotten to look up and beyond created things to You the powerful, good, wise, and generous Giver. Above all, we praise You for entering into creation by becoming Jesus Christ, full man yet fully God, who redeems us, mercifully recreates us by the Holy Spirit, and previews an even more glorious creation yet to be. Amen.

Make any necessary announcements and distribute study leaflet 2.

# Creation of Man and Woman

## Genesis 1:26; 2:18–25; Mark 10:1–9; Acts 17:16–31

*Preparing for the Session*

### Central Focus

God's highest creation on the earth is man and woman. They are created for fellowship with God. As God's representatives over creation, they are to cultivate the earth's resources and, with the attitude of mutual respect, care and provide for those different than themselves. Moreover, man and woman, as husband and wife, are to be faithful and of mutual service to each other as they reflect the love of God, who in Jesus Christ is shown to be self-giving. Through constant dependence upon the God of creative love and constant fellowship with Him through Jesus Christ, each person's life reaches its fullest meaning.

### Objectives

That participants, led by the Holy Spirit working through God's Word, will

1. appreciate the value each person has as a unique creation of God;

2. work toward giving respect and support to all members of the human family; and

3. cherish the cultural diversity on earth but not accept the plurality of religions that do not confess Jesus Christ as the only path to a blessed eternity as equal with Christianity.

**Note for the small-group leaders:** Lesson notes and other materials you will need begin on page 60.

### For the Lecture Leader

*Session Plan*

#### Worship

Begin the session with the hymn printed in the study leaflet. Accompaniments are available in denominational hymnals, such as *Lutheran Service Book* or *Lutheran Worship* (refer to hymnal index). (Note: Concordia Publishing House has available *The Concordia Organist.* All the initial worship hymns in the LifeLight courses are included in this resource. It's especially helpful for mission congregations and small parishes. See the list of study resources on page 7.) Follow with this prayer:

#### Prayer

Dear heavenly Father, pour down upon us the gift of Your Holy Spirit so that we may ever remain conscious of the unique dignity You have bestowed upon us by giving to us Your divine image. Because Your image was given to all human beings, help us to treat others with the respect that is theirs because You created and redeemed them. Call to our remembrance the significance of Your coming to earth to become the man Jesus Christ. May we as husband or wife learn how to daily and concretely exhibit Your self-giving love to each other. We pray this on the basis of Jesus' intercession. Amen.

### Lecture Presentation

#### Introduction

Are human beings merely small energy pockets in the vast field of all energy? Can human behavior be analyzed simply on the basis of pure material processes? Psychologists, sociologists, political scientists, neurosurgeons, philosophers, and theologians seek to answer the question each human also needs to know: "What is man?" (See Psalm 8:4 and Job 7:17.)

Does the answer start with the Genesis narrative of the creation of the first humans? Is Scripture true when it speaks of the creation of Adam as the first man? Jesus certainly thought so. He based His position on marriage on the Genesis account of God bringing Adam to Eve (Mark 10:7). In Romans 5:12–17, the apostle Paul draws a contrast between the disobedience of Adam and the obedience of Jesus. If Adam and Eve did not really exist, then Adam's act of disobedience would not be a historical event. And if Adam's act of disobedience did not really occur, then Paul's analogy about Jesus' act of obedience that benefits all humanity (2 Corinthians 5:19) would be meaningless.

## 1 The Creation of Adam (Genesis 1:26)

Scripture expresses in two ways the special place that humans have in creation. First, by the use of the word "then," and second, by the record of God taking counsel, saying, "Let Us make man." God did not say these words when creating earlier things. The Hebrew text records that the triune God said (literally), "Let Us make Adam." Scripture uses the word "Adam" in the plural. "Adam" is the generic name for the human race. Linguists think that the word "Adam" is derived from the verb *adam*, which means "to be red." The Hebrew word for "ground," *adamah*, also may be derived from the word for "red."

A human being is a unity of the physical and the spiritual. Genesis 2:7 states that the first man was constructed from soil (Hebrew *aphar*). While the ESV translation speaks of it as "dust," Luther calls it *Erdenkloss*, "lump of earth." Thus man has a definite connection to the earth, and the human body is dependent upon various elements in the earth for its health.

The human body is very valuable because it serves as the visible form of a person. Moreover, it is through a physical body that a believer can do the will of God on earth, as a "living sacrifice" (Romans 12:1), because the Holy Spirit enables the new spiritual life given to that body (1 Corinthians 3:16–17). However, Satan, in his attempt to dethrone God, wants humans to use God's gift of the human body as a demonic vehicle for doing evil in the world (Galatians 5:13).

The physical part of human nature was given additional dignity by the Son of God's incarnation as Jesus Christ, as well as by His bodily resurrection and His taking His glorified body into heaven. Jesus will finally affirm how valuable the body is when He gives all people a resurrection body that will remain with them throughout eternity (1 Corinthians 15:52).

However, God has given every person not only a material, visible body but also a spirit-soul (Matthew 27:50; Hebrews 12:23). Though theologians continue to debate whether the human spirit is different from the human soul, it can be said that either refers to the invisible side of what a person is. According to Genesis 2:7, when God breathed life into the clay He had shaped, the result was a living soul. When the spirit-soul inhibits a body, the material becomes a living human person.

The spirit-soul side of a human being continues to exist even at the time when the physical body becomes simply a corpse to be put in a grave. The person's life continues apart from the body and is with God until the Last Day, when Jesus will bring in the new creation and will clothe the believer's spirit-soul with a resurrected and glorious body (Matthew 10:28).

## 2 The Creation of Eve (Genesis 2:18–25)

Verse 18—Having created Adam, God said, "I will make him a helper fit for him." God created people to be social, to be in relationship both to other humans and to God. Man is to live in community, not in a self-centered solitude.

Verse 19—Then God brought all the animals before Adam and had him name them. This was an expression of Adam's lordship over the animals and showed Adam concretely that they were not suitable as equal companions for him.

Verses 21–23—After the naming, in a way that Adam was not allowed to see, a special work of divine creation took place. God willed that the sexes would become differentiated. God created Eve, a woman. Her creation was indeed special. She, like Adam, was created in the image of God. But as to the manner of her creation, she was made neither out of nothing (like the universe), nor directly out of "dust from the ground" (like Adam; Genesis 2:7), but out of Adam.

With the creation of Eve, Adam saw a reflection of himself, a complement to himself. God made for Adam a woman fully his equal. In this way, his loneliness was to be lessened. Woman was not created to be Adam's mere assistant ("helper"; v. 20). Some speak of woman as a "help meet" (KJV), which has the sense of the archaic English word *meet*, meaning the woman "fit to" or "corresponded to" the man. As an expression of his joy at God's creation of woman, Adam said, (v. 23) "This at last is bone of my bones and flesh of my flesh." "Bone of my bones" is a Hebrew idiom meaning a "very close relative," "one of us," or in effect, "my equal."

God has given distinctive functions to a man and to a woman. Equality of worth is not equivalent to identity of role. Although men and women are equal, they are not the same. Their equality is complementary, for Adam said of Eve, (v. 23) "She shall be called Woman, because she was taken out of Man."

Ephesians 5:23 speaks of man as the "head" of his wife. Adam was chosen to represent the human race, even as

Jesus represents the new creation (Romans 5:19). First Corinthians 11:3 compares the "headship" of man in relation to his wife to that of the Son of God to His heavenly Father. St. Paul writes, "I want you to understand that the head of every man is Christ, the head of a wife is her husband, and the head of Christ is God."

In John 4:34, Jesus said that His "food" was to do the will of Him who sent Him and to accomplish His heavenly Father's work. That work involved suffering upon a cross. The heavenly Father afterward exalted the Son as Lord over all because of His self-sacrifice (Philippians 2:4–11). In an analogous way, when the husband's "headship" is that of voluntary, responsible, self-sacrificing love toward his wife, she in turn renders respect and support to her husband's leadership.

Verse 25—Adam and Eve were naked but not ashamed. This means that they accepted each other's difference and each other's dependence on the other. Thus it is that to be a human person, one willingly lives in interdependence, not independence. This is similar to the relationship within the triune Godhead.

## 3 A Marriage Made in Heaven (Genesis 2:24)

Marriage is a holy estate that was instituted by God; it is not just a result of human social experimentation. Marriage is the God-created union of one man and one woman that is valued so highly that the apostle Paul compared it to Christ's intimate relationship with the Church (Ephesians 5:21–33). Scripture says that marriage is to be honored by all, and that those who forbid people to marry are false teachers misled by demonic spirits (Hebrews 13:4; 1 Timothy 4:1–3). Through marriage, God provides man and woman with companionship, love, and the gift of sexual intimacy (1 Corinthians 7:5; 1 Thessalonians 4:4–5) that becomes also God's method for the continuation of the human family (Genesis 1:28).

Immediately after He created Eve, God brought her to Adam, who recognized her as his God-given spouse. Scripture then comments, (Genesis 2:24) "Therefore a man shall leave his father and his mother and hold fast to his wife, and they shall become one flesh."

This verse outlines three important actions that go into the creation of a marriage in God's sight. A marriage exists in God's sight when a man *leaves* his parents, with a view not merely to living apart from them but with the intent to *"hold fast"* to his wife and become *one flesh* with her. The leaving and the holding fast belong together and are to take place in that order. The two words certify the replacement of one human relationship, that of child and parent, by another, namely, that of becoming husband and wife.

Theologians point out that there are some similarities between these relationships and that they contain physical, emotional, and social elements. The physical in one case is conception, birth, and nurture; in the other sexual intercourse. The emotional involves "growing up," the process of growing out of the dependence of childhood into the maturity of partnership. The social is children inheriting an already existent family unit, couples creating a new one.

However, at the same time, there is an essential dissimilarity between them. The biblical notion of becoming one "flesh" encompasses not merely the soft tissues of a person's body but also the entire person as "enfleshed," that is, the whole person as a physical being. Husband and wife are so completely joined in marriage that two lives have entered into a common life. The result is that the unity of husband and wife is deeper than the relationship of children to their parents. Not to be overlooked is that when a later biblical text, Deuteronomy 6:4, says that God is "one," it uses the Hebrew word *Echad*, which is the same word used in Genesis 2:24 to say that the husband and wife become "one" flesh. The husband-wife interconnection is so deep that New Testament epistles base many exhortations upon it. Both St. Paul, in 1 Corinthians 7:12–13, and St. Peter, in 1 Peter 3:1–2, encourage a Christian to stay with a presently unbelieving spouse because the Christian's lifestyle within the marriage can influence the spouse's spirituality.

The Genesis 2:24 words "a man . . . *his* wife" underscore that the marriage union is an exclusive *man-woman* relationship. This includes making that relationship public at a social event ("leave his father and his mother"). Additionally, the marriage is entered into as one that is to be permanent ("hold fast to his wife"), and is consummated by sexual intercourse ("they shall become one flesh"). Any sexual relationship that deviates from God's revealed intention comes under divine judgment. Such deviations include polygamy (which contradicts the one man–one woman principle), cohabitation and clandestine unions (which involve no decisive public leaving of parents), casual encounters and temporary liaisons, and adultery. Homosexual partnerships violate the Bible's statement that "a man" shall be united to "his wife." Moreover, many divorces contradict God's word about "hold fast" and violate Jesus' prohibition "let not man separate" (Matthew 19:6).

## 4 "What Therefore God Has Joined Together, Let Not Man Separate" (Mark 10:1–9)

To God, marriage has the binding nature of a contract that demands faithfulness. While human laws establish the legal basis both for marriage and its breakdown (divorce), God is also involved in this intimate relationship between a man and a woman. As God incarnate upon earth, Jesus asserts this truth.

Verse 1—As Jesus headed toward His crucifixion, He left Galilee "and went to the region of Judea and beyond the Jordan." This region was under the jurisdiction of the ruler Herod Antipas. He was the one who beheaded John the Baptizer because he condemned Herod's adulterous relationship with his stepbrother's wife (Matthew 14:1–12). "Beyond the Jordan" is also the region where Moses gave the law that permitted divorce and remarriage because of the stubborn hearts of the people (Deuteronomy 24:1–4).

Verses 2–9—Some Pharisees then approached Jesus with a "test" question on divorce, a topic about which they themselves were in disagreement. It would be as controversial as if you asked an American politician, "Where do you stand on abortion?" Jesus' critics want to trick Him into saying something that would get Him in trouble with the ruler, Herod Antipas, who would hear about and maybe respond to Jesus as violently as he had to John the Baptizer. They asked, "Is it lawful for a man to divorce his wife?"

If Jesus answered yes, He would have discredited Himself for a lax interpretation of the Law (Deuteronomy 24:1–4). On the other hand, if Jesus answered no, He would have insulted Herod Antipas, who had divorced his wife.

But always in control of every situation, Jesus presented a counter-question. He asked the Pharisees if they had not read what God, speaking through Moses, said about marriage originally.

Thinking they knew Scripture better than Jesus, the Pharisees immediately pointed out that Moses permitted a husband to write "a certificate of divorce" and thereby divorce her (Mark 10:4).

Jesus pointed out (v. 5) that Moses allowed divorce simply as a concession to the "hardness" of the human heart. Actually, the purpose of the "certificate of divorce" was not to authorize divorce but merely to limit its consequences for the woman. Without that document, she could later have been charged with adultery if she remarried—and then be punished by being stoned to death.

Jesus then referred back to God's real commandment on the subject. As the Son of God is faithful to His Bride, the Church (Ephesians 5:25), likewise husband and wife are to be faithful to each other. The union of husband and wife is no mere human convention, but it is a bond that God Himself made (Malachi 2:14–16) and which no one is authorized to dissolve. Hence Jesus' solemn declaration, (Mark 10:9) "What therefore God has joined together, let not man separate."

Jesus is well aware of the conflicts that two persons, both infected with sin, have in living together in the intimacy of marriage. For sinful humans, commitment to fidelity in marriage is not easy. Mutual forgiveness is vital to the maintenance of a good marriage. Jesus leaves no "loop holes" in His expectation that the Christian life is to be governed by the giving and receiving of forgiveness (Matthew 18:35). The Bride of Christ, the Church, lives daily under His forgiveness (Ephesians 5:26), and the "first" church, the Christian home, is to do so as well. As St. Paul wrote, (Ephesians 5:32–33) "This mystery is profound, and I am saying that it refers to Christ and the church. However, let each one of you love his wife as himself, and let the wife see that she respects her husband."

Thus, Jesus brings His teachings on suffering, self-denial, humility, and service into its most concrete and intimate sphere of human life: marriage. Within its intimacy, those trusting in Christ will also experience within their home the coming of His kingdom with power (Mark 9:1).

## 5 One Race and One Savior (Acts 17:16–31)

Verses 16–17—When the apostle Paul visited the multicultural city of Athens, its many pagan temples and statues provoked a great indignation in him. Each Sabbath, Paul preached in the synagogue, but the rest of the week he directly evangelized any pagan willing to listen to him in the marketplace.

Verse 18—In Paul's audience were some philosophers who considered Paul to be a mere "babbler," a speaker without a well-developed system of thought. Some other hearers considered Paul to be a propagandist for an unknown cult of "Jesus and the resurrection."

Verses 22–28—Paul responded with a reminder that all nations have their origin in "one," that is, Adam (v. 26). In God's sight, there is only one race. Even biological anthropology now recognizes that there isn't one gene, characteristic, or trait that distinguishes race. Even before Paul's message, Scripture testified that God made all people equal from the womb and that He will judge us if we treat any person unjustly (Job 31:13–15). Jesus was not "swayed by appearances" (Mark 12:14). He defended the worth of all, especially women, the disabled, and the elderly. Moreover, God reminded Peter that he "should not call any person common or unclean" (Acts 10:28).

No particular group of people can claim a superior origin over that of any other group. Scripture condemns any type of conduct or words that puts a person either at a disadvantage or advantage because of his or her color, culture, or ethnic origin. Such ethnocentrism (better word than *racism* because there is only one "race," the human race) is unacceptable because it attacks the unique dignity God has given to all human persons in having created them and, above all, having offered them reconciliation with Him through Christ.

Verses 26–27a—Nevertheless, while Christians acknowledge cultural diversity and appreciate whatever is good in the various cultures on the planet, Scripture forbids the acceptance of religious pluralism. This is what Paul points out to the Athenians. (V. 26) The God of creation is the Lord of history, who controls the rise and fall of nations. (V. 27a) God's governance of all nations is that people may seek Him and "might feel their way toward Him." Seeking God means relinquishing trust in mere human beings and in all that is not God (Isaiah 31:1), and turning to the only righteous, living God (Isaiah 55:7).

Verses 27b–31—God is "not far from each one of us." (V. 28) He is as close as the breath of life within us. (V. 30) Though God did not, in His providential goodness, destroy Athens for its idolatry, He commanded all people to a total reorientation regarding the Creator. (V. 31) He did this because a unique person has appeared on earth to begin a new era for all people. The turning point of history is Jesus. Salvation for all people is connected to only one name: "Jesus" (Acts 4:12).

## Conclusion

The Sacred Scripture reveals that humans are created beings, dependent upon the triune God and interdependent upon one another.

In biblical thought, a person's self-worth is not based on his "net worth." The dignity of a person is what he or she is intrinsically, a human created by God. Psalm 8:5 notes that each human person is "a little lower than the heavenly beings" (some ancient text has "a little lower than God"). For this reason, human persons are to be protected as the highest life form on earth (Genesis 9:6).

At the same time, the Christian Church, and its most basic unit, the family, is to mentor to its culture the self-sacrificing love that a Christian husband and wife have toward each other. In such marital love, Christians give concrete witness to the saving love that the triune God intends to bring to all cultures through their trust in the only one who benefits humanity eternally, Jesus Christ.

## Concluding Activities

Pray aloud: Dear heavenly Father, we thank You for the dignity You have bestowed upon us by creating us in Your image. Send upon us the gift of Your Holy Spirit that He may enable us to exhibit Your reconciling love in Jesus Christ in our homes, our marriages, and the way that we treat those who are different from us. Keep us all in faith in Jesus Christ as we look forward with hope and expectation to when many more of the human race are brought into the one family of Your redeemed children. Amen.

Make any necessary announcements and distribute study leaflet 3.

# God's Invisible Creation

## Matthew 4:1–11; Ephesians 6:10–20

*Preparing for the Session*

## Central Focus

The Creator is so powerful and generous that He created various personal beings who do not require physical bodies or visibility to be complete. The Creator is also the loving Father who protects humanity from certain invisible persons in His creation that seek humanity's destruction. Their defeat by God is certain, and He wants humanity to use His weapons and thereby participate in that victory.

## Objectives

That participants, led by the Holy Spirit working through God's Word, will

1. appreciate the generosity of God in bringing an invisible creation into existence;
2. be realistic about the danger of the invisible demonic kingdom to God's people; and
3. actively join with God in using His weapons that defeat the agents of evil in creation.

**Note for the small-group leaders:** Lesson notes and other materials you will need begin on page 62.

## For the Lecture Leader

*Session Plan*

### Worship

Begin the session with the hymn printed in the study leaflet. Accompaniments are available in denominational hymnals, such as *Lutheran Service Book* or *Lutheran Worship* (refer to hymnal index). (Note: Concordia Publishing House has available *The Concordia Organist*. All the initial worship hymns in the LifeLight courses are included in this resource. It's especially helpful for mission congregations and small parishes. See the list of study resources on page 7.) Follow with this prayer:

### Prayer

Blessed are You, O Lord, king of the universe both visible and invisible. Blessed are You! We come again to You in worship and in praise for Your multiple gifts to us, especially the gift of Your angels, who bring us Your multiple blessings. Give us the eyes of faith to appreciate their ministry. Continue to surround us with them that they may be among our defenses against our spiritual enemies. In the name of Jesus Christ, the one whom angels worship, we offer our petition. Amen.

## Lecture Presentation

### Introduction

Like an ocean traveler who when beholding a floating iceberg is seeing only a part of its mass, so also we see only a little of what God has created. The Nicene Creed confesses our belief in the God who created all things "visible and invisible."

### 1 The Heavenly Hosts

Throughout Scripture, God is referred to as "the Lord of hosts" (Psalm 84:1, 3, 12). The term *hosts* means "armies." Though God is all-powerful, He has created armies of beings to carry out His will in creation. Scripture uses various terms for these heavenly servants. The broadest term is *angel*, which means "messenger." The context helps a Scripture reader determine whether a particular use of "angel" is referring to a messenger from heaven or a human messenger. (In Matthew 11:10, the word translated as "messenger" could also be translated as "angel.")

Scripture does not pinpoint the day within creation when these special heavenly messengers were created. Since angels are part of the order of creation (Colossians 1:16), it holds that they were created within the Creation days of Genesis 1. Because Psalm 91:11 informs us that one of the ministries of the good angels is to support human life, then we may surmise that all the angels were created before God's creation of Adam.

The material universe is made of substance—subatomic particles, at least. However, angels, understood in the narrow sense of the term, are extra-cosmic persons who are not a part of a universe of matter. They are spirits

(Hebrews 1:14). As spirits, they are unique heavenly persons who do not require visibility in order to exist (Numbers 22:31; 2 Kings 6:16–17; Colossians 1:16a).

As individual persons, angels have names (Luke 1:26). They are self-aware, with the power to think, and they have emotions (Luke 15:7). For example, in Luke 1:12–13, 29–30, we see how the angel Gabriel interacted with Zechariah and the Virgin Mary.

When God desired them to do so, some of God's supernatural messengers appeared so humanlike that the humans they visited did not recognize them as supernatural visitors. The military leader Gideon talked with an angel but did not know it was an angel until the angel set a rock on fire (Judges 6:21–22). Samson's parents, however, were quite aware that an angel had visited them (Judges 13:6).

There are numerous angels (Psalm 68:17). Gradations of rank appear to exist among the angels, since Scripture mentions archangels (Jude 9; 1 Thessalonians 4:16). Evidently, the term *archangel* refers to those angels, such as Michael, who are of a higher rank than others.

When Adam and Eve sinned and were cast out of Eden, God used cherubim to prevent their reentrance (Genesis 3:24). Cherubim are also mentioned in connection with the design of the ark of the covenant that God had the Israelites construct during Moses' era (Exodus 25:10–22). The ark was a gold-covered wooden chest. On its top, over the solid gold lid called the "mercy seat," were the two cherubim, shaped liked humans but with wings instead of arms. Their outstretched wings touched each other (Exodus 25:20). The space between the wings and over the mercy seat was considered the sacred space of God on earth (1 Samuel 4:4; Psalm 99:1).

Another special heavenly creation is a seraph (Hebrew word meaning "burning one"). The prophet Isaiah was in the Jerusalem temple when he beheld seraphim (Isaiah 6:2). Each had six wings, two covering the face, two covering the feet, and two for flying. This is all that the Bible says about the seraphim.

Saint Paul refers to other types of heavenly beings under the mysterious general terms "rulers," "authorities," "thrones," and "dominions" (Romans 8:38; Ephesians 3:10; Colossians 1:16).

## 2 The Ministries of God's Good Angels

The good angels' ministry is essentially working so that God's will be done on earth as it is in heaven (Hebrews 1:14). Because God used some angels to deliver His moral Law for humanity through Moses (Galatians 3:19), angels are sometimes thought of as God's "secret agents," His police officers for cosmic order.

Moreover, as agents of order, God's good angels have a ministry to nations as they work to prevent anarchy. They defend magistrates whom God desires to remain in power, as when God defended Daniel (Daniel 6:22). Angels also ward off dangers and destroy the enemies of God's people (Acts 12:23).

God cares so much for His servants that His good angels carry out various ministries to them (Job 1:10; Psalm 34:7). The heavenly angels even pray for the community of believers on earth (Isaiah 62:6–7; Revelation 5:8).

The heavenly angels delight in praising God (Job 38:7; Revelation 5:8–14). Therefore, the angels are present at earthly worship services and hope to see them reflecting the orderliness of heaven (see Hebrews 12:22–29).

God's angels are with believers from their Baptism, through childhood and adulthood, and even until their death. Angels can miraculously protect a person from physical harm (Psalm 91:12; Hebrews 1:14). However, angels do not rescue a person who deliberately does something foolish. Satan tempted Jesus to throw Himself down from the top of a temple pinnacle for angels to catch. Jesus rebuked Satan for this suggestion (Matthew 4:5–7).

God will use His angels to announce the ending of the present form of creation (Matthew 24:31). After Jesus pronounces His final judgment upon all humanity, the good angels will carry out God's punishment upon the damned (Matthew 13:41–42), who will be separated from the presence of the saved (Matthew 25:31–32). Joyfully, God's angels will escort His people to the blessings of the new creation (Matthew 25:46).

## 3 Evil Hosts

The first two chapters of Genesis describe creation and its various parts in harmony with God. The heavenly choir sings in harmony under its Master Director. But suddenly, Genesis 3 describes a rebellion, and the dissonance of sin appears. An evil personal power takes what was a beautiful creature—a snake—and turns it into a slithering instrument of deception and death.

Scripture does not specify the time when some angels

first rebelled against God. It must have occurred between the time when God completed the work of creation and the fall of Adam and Eve into sin.

There is a chief of the evil angels (Luke 11:15) who is described by many names. His most common name, Satan (Job 1:6; Acts 5:3), is derived from a Hebrew verb that means "to be or act as an adversary." The word was also used to refer to a person who brings an accusation against another person in a court of law (Psalm 59:1). Its Greek New Testament equivalent means "accuser" (Revelation 12:10).

This "accuser" is also known as "the devil" (Greek *diabolos*, "slanderer," "whisperer"; Matthew 4:1) because he attempts to get humans to accept his false statements about God. Often, what the devil does is used as a title for him: "tempter" (1 Thessalonians 3:5); "murderer" (John 8:44); "deceiver" (Revelation 12:9).

Though Scripture says little about what the devil's first sin was, there is indirect evidence that spiritual lust—the desire to be above God and humans—characterized Satan's sin. The Epistle of Jude (v. 6) says that the evil angels "did not stay within their own position of authority, but left their proper dwelling." Satan and his cohorts rebelled against the order in creation God had assigned to them.

Though there is only one Satan, there are demons (wicked angels) under his control (Matthew 25:41). Scripture does not state their number. If wicked angels are identified with demons, then their number is great (Mark 5:9). Through them, Satan gains information and implements his will. Zechariah 13:2 and Acts 8:7 speak of them as "unclean spirits"; this title describes their impure nature.

Scripture does not paint a ridiculous portrait of Satan as a man in red flannel underwear with horns, a tail, and a pitchfork. Such caricaturés are part of Satan's wiles to delude us into thinking that he does not exist. But Satan and his demons are dangerous beings. He and his cohorts disguise themselves as angels of light (2 Corinthians 11:14). Christians are to be realistic about the presence of personal, spiritual evil among them. God invites His people to take up the God-supplied weapons to resist them in order to participate in God's victory over them.

## 4 The War with Evil (Matthew 4:1–11)

Jesus told His followers to petition God to "lead us not into temptation, but deliver us from evil (or "the evil one"; Matthew 6:13). Since God leads no one to sin (James 1:13), what Jesus is teaching in His prayer is that only God can prevent the destruction of His people when evil attacks them (consult Luke 22:31–32). Satan thinks that the only way to shame God is to alienate us from Him. To accomplish this, Satan becomes the "father of lies" (John 8:44) and the supreme accuser of God and man. As "the deceiver of the whole world" (Revelation 12:9) and slanderer (devil), he uses various methods to attempt to convince people that God does not want to give heaven's best gifts to those He created.

Satan's words to Eve, (Genesis 3:5) "For God knows that when you eat of it your eyes will be opened, and you will be like God, knowing good and evil," were a direct attack on God's goodness and an appeal to Eve's pride. The devil portrayed God as denying Adam and Eve the one thing that would bring them ultimate fulfillment: equality with God. The first human couple fell to the satanic lie, and they thereby put a fray in their lifeline with God, the source of life in its abundance. The obvious result was biological and, eventually, spiritual death—if God had not given them the first promise of salvation (Genesis 3:15).

Verse 1—Centuries later, humanity's arch-adversary tried again; this time he tested the new representative of the human race, Jesus Christ (Romans 5:15). At His Baptism, Jesus was acknowledged by God the Father as His Son. After Jesus was baptized, the Holy Spirit led Him into unoccupied land west of the Jordan River. There, Jesus was "field-tested" by the devil (Matthew 4:1). As Jesus was about to begin His ministry to save humanity, the devil tested Him three times; two of the tests began with the words "If You are the Son of God . . ." Having successfully used that logic on Adam and Eve, Satan hoped it would also lead to Jesus' disobedience of His heavenly Father's plan.

Verses 2–3—Having fasted throughout the forty days in the wilderness, Jesus' physical hunger was great. The devil presented Jesus with a temptation that took into account the reality of His humanity. The Judean desert was dotted with small round stones that resembled the pancake-shaped loaves of bread common in the Middle East. The devil said to Jesus, "If You are the Son of God, command these stones to become loaves of bread." The "if" has the sense of "since."

The devil was testing whether Jesus would use His unique Sonship in a self-serving way, rather than following Scripture's advice to "wait patiently for Him [the Lord]" (Psalm 37:7). It is quite possible that the devil was suggesting to Jesus that His Father was keeping something back from Him.

Verse 4—Using the "sword" of the Spirit, Jesus rebuked the tempter with a quote from Deuteronomy 8:3. It reminds us that just as children are not sustained by food or clothing, but by their parents who furnish these things, so it is that humankind is sustained ultimately by God, who is the source of everything.

Verses 5–6—Satan likes the spectacular, so he suggested to Jesus that He do something that would be a visible display of power. After all, that is the type of leader people like. The devil took Jesus to the Jerusalem temple to stand on one of the sanctuary's high towers. By leaping down from the temple's pinnacle and landing unharmed, Jesus would have presented Himself as a uniquely powerful leader. To support this dramatic display, the devil cleverly seized upon Jesus' desire to exhibit a total trust in His heavenly Father. The devil quoted Psalm 91:11–12—but incompletely and out of context. He left out the phrase "in all your ways." A deliberate throwing of oneself from a temple pinnacle would not correspond to an accidental stumbling over a stone in one's path, as that psalm's context described.

Verse 7—Jesus corrected the devil by quoting Deuteronomy 6:16: "Again it is written, 'You shall not put the Lord your God to the test'" (Matthew 4:7). God did not give His promises to be used for selfish ends.

Verses 8–9—Finally, the devil took Jesus to a high mountain to provide Him with a vision of worldly kingdoms. The devil claimed that he could fulfill the promise given to God's chosen in Psalm 2:8: "Ask of me, and I will make the nations your heritage, and the ends of the earth your possession" (see Matthew 4:8–9). But the tempter's claim is false, because everything of earth is the Lord's (Psalm 24:1; 50:12). Nevertheless, the self-serving devil asked that Jesus bow down and worship him.

Verse 10—Jesus abruptly responded with words from Deuteronomy 6:13 that assert God's sovereignty and the need to serve God alone. While the devil had said nothing explicitly about service, nevertheless, whatever humans truly worship they will also serve.

Verse 11—After Jesus' wilderness victory over the devil, some good angels came and ministered to their Lord. Probably, they gave Jesus food. Thus, Jesus' later words to His followers, (Matthew 6:33) "But seek first the kingdom of God and His righteousness, and all these things will be added to you" were fulfilled.

## 5 Defenses against the Evil Hosts (Ephesians 6:10–20)

God guaranteed ancient Israel they would have His promised land (Deuteronomy 1:8); but first they would have to do battle with an enemy to enjoy that land, and do so confident in the Lord's might (Joshua 1:9–18).

In like manner, the words of Romans 8:37 assure Christians they can be confident of the good news that because of Christ they will reach the new land Christ promises His followers. However, on their journey through this life toward that land, Christ has not removed them from having to fight off that which would try to steal their victory. St. Paul encouraged Timothy to fight the good fight for the faith (1 Timothy 6:12). Ephesians 6:10–20 details how God supplies His "Christian soldiers" with His weapons to remain victorious. Indeed, Isaiah 59:17 reminds us that God Himself is the armor.

The apostle Paul gives this comforting word: (1 Corinthians 10:13) "God is faithful, and He will not let you be tempted beyond your ability, but with the temptation He will also provide the way of escape, that you may be able to endure it." God provides four special "doors of escape."

The first defense God supplies His people is Door 1. The sign over the door reads "Fire Escape." It invites a person to make a strategic retreat. Temptation is not to be *fed* but rather *fled*, as Joseph did from Pharaoh's adulterous wife (Genesis 39:11–12). Similar advice is given in 1 Corinthians 6:18. And Ephesians 4:27 says, "Give no opportunity to the devil." When God's people draw near Him, the demons run in the opposite direction.

Next is Door 2. The sign over this door reads "Chapel." It opens to a place of prayer. Jesus encourages Christians to flee to God through fervent prayer when they recognize that they are under spiritual attack (Matthew 26:41; Ephesians 6:18a). This indicates their trust in His promise that He will rescue them from the evil one.

God also supplies His people with Door 3. The sign over this door reads "Armory." Inside is a sword and a shield. The sword is Scripture (Ephesians 6:17), made by the Holy Spirit, which Jesus also used (Matthew 4:4, 6, 10). Satan will use people's ignorance of God's Word to deceive them so that they overlook how Christ frees them to be His heirs (John 8:31–32) rather than Satan's captives.

Believers march forward into victory with not only the sword of the Spirit in one hand but also with the body-length shield in the other. This shield also comes from behind Door 3, and it quenches the fiery darts of Satan (Ephesians 6:16). It is the shield of faith, which focuses upon Jesus as the sinner's forgiving Savior, the only protection that deflects satanic arrows of accusations and deceptions about what they have become in Christ. The foundation under this door is Jesus Christ, the "strong man" (Luke 11:20–22) and Savior of sinners (Psalm 19:5; Isaiah 53:12). Through Him, the believer is enabled to stand firm in the Lord's victory.

The accusations of Satan and the wicked angels against believers at God's bar of justice are thrown out of heaven's "court" because believers in Jesus Christ have in Him their eternal advocate (John 12:31–32; Romans 8:1, 33–34; Revelation 12:7, 11).

We now come to the final door: Door 4. The sign over this door reads "Assistants." For certain struggles in life, the advice, counsel, and encouragement of consecrated Christian friends are of great help. Even ten-month-old toddlers must be encouraged to firmly plant their little feet, one in front of the other, and begin walking. The toddler's parents' consistent, loving, cheering presence moves the child to start the walk. Complete trust in the parent, but measured cautions in his or her own little ability, moves the child forward.

Jesus' followers are often called His "children" (John 1:12). He is well aware of their difficulties, doubts, and discouragement that accompany their spiritual growth (John 14:1). Therefore, God puts the lonely Christian warrior into a community of His people who will exhort and encourage one another to continue the fight (Hebrews 10:25; James 5:16; 1 Peter 5:9). As the Church gathers around God's Word and Sacraments, God sees to it that His Church survives the attacks from hell's agents (Matthew 16:18).

## Conclusion

God has an invisible creation, nonhumans, some of whom are on the side of humanity, while others seek their destruction. There is no Christian discipleship apart from conflict with evil. Victory comes to those who, while wearing God's armor, reject any compromise with Satan.

Having entered the dimension of time and space, God, in Christ, allows people to see a reality greater than their present fallen world. This new vision replaces Satan's illusions and lies (John 1:9–10; Hebrews 2:14–15). Jesus has already conquered their enemy, so they can move into the victory He has already obtained for them.

## Concluding Activities

Pray aloud: Dear heavenly Father, thank You for giving us the words of Scripture, through which the Holy Spirit opens our spiritual eyes to see the many assistants You have given us for our walk in faith to Your eternal home. Keep us focused on Jesus Christ, the historical proof that You have given to us heaven's greatest gift and that Satan lies when he insinuates that You are not on our side. Enable each of us to be Your messengers of encouragement by word, letter, and action to any downtrodden believer among us this day. With all the heavenly host, we exalt Your holy name. Amen.

Make any necessary announcements and distribute study leaflet 4.

# God Is Still Creator

## Acts 7; Luke 11:5–13; 12:22–34

*Preparing for the Session*

## Central Focus

God remains in contact with every part of creation and with every person within it. Nothing happens without His control. God's control demonstrates His power and wisdom and also the faithfulness and care of a loving Father, despite the presence of evil and suffering now in creation, as He wisely moves it forward to a new creation. At the same time, humans are not robots under His power but have been given the ability to respond in faith to His promises and to be accountable to their Creator.

## Objectives

That participants, led by the Holy Spirit working through God's Word, will

1. acknowledge that God continues to direct, uphold, and enable all that He has created;
2. be confident that when they seek God's help in prayer, His answer will be for their welfare; and
3. focus on Jesus as God's deep love that redeems and moves the world toward a new creation.

**Note for the small-group leaders:** Lesson notes and other materials you will need begin on page 64.

## For the Lecture Leader

*Session Plan*

### Worship

Begin the session with the hymn printed in the study leaflet. Accompaniments are available in denominational hymnals, such as *Lutheran Service Book* or *Lutheran Worship* (refer to hymnal index). (Note: Concordia Publishing House has available *The Concordia Organist.* All the initial worship hymns in the LifeLight courses are included in this resource. It's especially helpful for mission congregations and small parishes. See the list of study resources on page 7.) Follow with this prayer:

### Prayer

O most Holy Trinity, Lord, Preserver and Redeemer of all creation, open our eyes to see and our hearts to appreciate that You are still working among us. May we not mistake Your working behind the scenes in every budding of a flower, birth of a child, or delivering of redemption through Word and Sacrament as evidence that You are not actively working to restore creation to its fullness. In moments of joy or tremendous sadness, dear heavenly Father, point us to the Christ of the cross, whose love for us Your Holy Spirit uses to sustain us. On the basis of Jesus' name, Savior, we offer this prayer. Amen.

## Lecture Presentation

### Introduction

Creation is not closed to its Creator's continuing action in it, because the existence of every part of creation depends upon God's power and will. The triune God is the ultimate sustainer and shaper of all that exists. Some people make a mistake by focusing on the chronological aspect of creation, asking such questions as when and how the world began in the distant past.

However, God's past action of creating the universe is not the only significant aspect of the Creator's relationship to it. God is still involved in the rise and fall of nations (Acts 17:26) and in every aspect of every person's life, from the womb (Isaiah 44:2) to the tomb (Psalm 23:4).

### 1 God Is Still Creator (Acts 7)

Nothing on earth can continue to exist without God's involvement. Psalm 65:9–10 notes that God visits the earth so that it can bring forth crops and people can gather a bountiful harvest. Certainly, human beings have a responsibility to clear, plow, irrigate, reap, and thresh to get that harvest. But, according to Genesis 1, God made the earth fruitful and created nature before Adam was told to fill and subdue the earth. All human acts of cultivation would be fruitless if God had not already established the processes of nature, "blessing its growth."

However, God's vision of creation involves more than fruitful soil. Even before God created the universe, He had a plan for it that involved the Son of God (Ephesians 1:3–6; Colossians 1:16–17). Therefore, sin's corruption of the earth and humans did not take God by surprise.

Psalm 65:5 writes of the "awesome" activity of God within creation that is connected to God's righteousness. This awesome activity is the divine rescue that gives "the hope of all the ends of the earth" for earth's restoration to a physical and spiritual wholeness. God calls His people, many of whom became "heroes of faith" (Hebrews 11), to trust Him and join Him in that exciting movement.

Sadly, God's people often hesitated to do so. They wanted to stay with familiar traditions they created around Moses and Jerusalem. But God wanted them to move on so that they could be His light in a wider world (Acts 1:8). When they hesitated, God used persecution to get them moving outside of the confines of Jerusalem (Acts 8:1).

Acts 7—The deacon Stephen castigated people who were frozen in old ways of thinking and didn't want to move forward with God. His plan for creation is such that it breaks through prejudices connected to our narrow visions of who and what is important in life (vv. 48–50). God's plan for creation is so vast that it involves all people on earth and is connected to God's gift to them of a "Promised Land" that will eventually be seen in its eternal dimensions.

Verse 2—Stephen spoke first of God's gracious call to Abraham. He was a man who came from the pagan territory of Mesopotamia and the ancient city of Ur (Genesis 11:31). Abram ("the father is exalted") was renamed by God as Abraham ("father of a multitude of nations"; Genesis 17:5). That name would help Abraham remember God's promises to him.

Verses 3–4—As God moved His plans for creation and its people forward, He called those He would bless to move forward with Him, even though it would mean hardship for them, such as leaving the comfortable and the familiar ("your land"; "your kindred") to walk with God. He would lead them into a future, into a "land" known fully only by God Himself, which, as He said, "I will show you." God moved Abraham from his home into what is today Palestine but was once called Canaan (Genesis 12:5).

Verses 5–8—Abraham was a man of faith (Hebrews 11:8), during his lifetime his earthly eyes did not see the fulfillment of all that God had promised him. The only land he possessed was his burial plot in Canaan. Though God promised Abraham many heirs, he had no children until God miraculously intervened to give the elderly Sarah her first child, Isaac (Genesis 21:1–3; Hebrews 11:11). But by God commanding Abraham to practice a ritual circumcision, Abraham had a visible reminder that God had made him and his descendents recipients of God's blessings.

Verses 9–16—Next, Stephen presents a summary of God's wondrous intervention in the life of Joseph, one of Abraham's descendants. Through the twists and turns of his life, Joseph retained the faith that God had given him. God's intervention in Joseph's life brought him from pit and prison to the palace of Pharaoh and power (told in Genesis 37–50). Trusting that God can work good for His people in the midst of their suffering on His behalf, Joseph told his brothers that God had sent him into Egypt as a way of preserving their life (Genesis 45:4–5; 50:19–21).

Despite his long and prosperous life, Joseph looked forward, not back when he told his brothers, (Genesis 50:25) "God will surely visit you." Always confident that his moves were under God's guidance, Joseph's last words pointed confidently toward a more wondrous future under God (Genesis 50:24–25). Joseph asked that his bones be carried from Egypt to Canaan. Joseph recognized that Egypt's material prosperity was not God's ultimate blessing to him and his descendants. In the future, God again would work outside the confines of Palestine to free the Israelites through Moses and the exodus from Egypt.

What happened to Joseph in ancient Egypt was a preview of what happened to Jesus, the "son" of another Joseph. Joseph and Jesus were both rejected by their kinsmen. But Joseph and Jesus trusted the will of the heavenly Father, who eventually led them to become rescuers, blessings to others.

## 2 God's Continuing Care Encourages Persistent Prayer (Luke 11:5–13)

Jesus tells a humorous story of a persistent neighbor in order to encourage His followers to continue in prayer, because even they became discouraged at times.

Verses 5–7—Jesus speaks of a certain man, who, while asleep at home, is awakened by the unexpected arrival of a friend on a journey. Having traveled a long way, the visitor was in need of rest and food. Hospitality was considered a sacred duty in the Middle East, so naturally the traveler expected provisions when he came to his friend's house. Since the householder did not have extra provisions for an unexpected guest, he, in turn, visited his neighbor for assistance. But he found the door shut—a "do not disturb" sign in the ancient East. But he didn't let that stop him; he proceeded to shamelessly rouse his neighbor with the plea to lend him three loaves of bread (small round loaves that were an adequate meal for one person).

Verse 8—The neighbor was hesitant to respond to this request. His whole family was sleeping close together on a raised platform in their one-room house, so he would have to climb over other family members to get to the door, thus waking them. Yet, if he did not get up, the continued knocking would eventually waken the family anyway. Nevertheless, where friendship did not prevail in this situation, persistence on the part of the knocker did.

Verses 9–10—From this humorous story, Jesus led into a discussion of God's willingness to give to those who "ask," "seek," and "knock" for His assistance. God wants His people to pray persistently, but not because He is unwilling to answer their prayers. The whole context makes it clear that God cares about the needs of those He created and is eager to aid the needy: (v. 10) "For everyone who asks receives, and the one who seeks finds, and to the one who knocks it will be opened." However, if God's people do not want what they are asking for enough to be persistent, then they do not sincerely desire it. Persistence helps a person both understand and express the intensity of his or her need. Above all, it aids the one in need to recognize and appreciate the importance of the giving God in their lives.

Verses 11–13a—Using a line of reasoning that moves from the lesser to the greater, Jesus contrasts an earthly father with the heavenly Father. If persistence rouses an unwilling neighbor, then "how much more" will persistence in prayer move God to respond to His earthly children?

An earthly father will not give his children things that are either deceptive (a small snake that looked like the fish the child asked for) or harmful (such as a scorpion). Certainly then, the good and wise heavenly Father will respond to His spiritual children's needs, even though they are "evil," and give to them whatever is helpful to their eternal well-being, especially the Holy Spirit. When Jesus says, (v. 13a) "If you then, who are evil, know how to give good gifts to your children," He is expounding on the truth regarding the universal sin-condition of every human heart.

Verse 13b—Jesus also speaks of God's gift of the Holy Spirit. In the time of the Old Testament, the Holy Spirit came to a select few to give them special earthly abilities. But in the messianic age, as Joel 2 had predicted, God's Spirit comes to all of God's people to create faith in Jesus Christ (1 Corinthians 12:3) and to motivate their prayer life (Romans 8:26–27).

## 3 God's Continuing Care Conquers Anxiety (Luke 12:22–34)

Verse 22—Jesus' followers at times get "anxious" (the Greek word used here means "to be torn apart"). They get out of focus over food and clothing—how to gain more or how to protect from losing what they have.

Verses 22–34—Certainly, Jesus expects His followers to be prudent, working hard while on earth. But as in Jesus' parable about the foolish farmer (Luke 12:13–21), those wise in Christ know He has not failed to prepare them for the life after death. Not to plan for life beyond the grave is disastrous because, as Jesus says, (v. 23) "life is more than food, and the body more than clothing." Jesus exhorts Christians to not devote their time to laboring for perishable things but to the food that endures eternally, and which He gives them (John 6:27). Having provided for our eternal life through Jesus Christ, God certainly cares about our life now in earthly time.

Verse 24—Jesus wants His people to see that anxiety is fed by a false security and a deceptive view of life and of God. The antidote to the poison of anxiety is trust in the caring God of creation. God feeds the ravens that do not struggle for things. Human beings are of greater value than such birds.

Verses 25–26—Jesus asks, "Which of you by being anxious can add a single hour to his span of life? If then you are not able to do as small a thing as that, why are you anxious about the rest?" (Consult also Psalm 39:5.) Anxiety is illogical because it does not accomplish anything. Anxiety does not empty tomorrow of its sorrow, but it does empty from one's sight the beauty and strength of the God who cares for those He created.

Verses 27–28—God not only provides humans with their basic needs but He also gives beauty to their life. God supplies the beauty of the lilies of the field. Their dazzling color, more glorious than the clothing of a king, is not the product of human hard work, such as was reflected in the colored robes of King Solomon. Lilies do not have to "toil or spin" to get their glory.

Jesus' talk about birds and flowers is not sentimental gibberish. He knows that birds die and flowers wither. Moreover, Scripture says Christians are to work for their daily bread and not be lazy (2 Thessalonians 3:6–15). What Jesus is doing is encouraging Christians to exercise faith in their caring God. Focusing upon Him enables Christians to battle against debilitating anxiety. Since God continues to take care of "unclean" (in rabbis' ritual laws) ravens, and because God paints the beauty upon the lilies, despite their brief life span, then "how much more" will God provide a truly beautiful life for His people. Jesus, therefore, chastises His followers: "O you of little faith!" A "little" faith is a faith that is not making much use of its power. Thus, Jesus is telling them that they need to put their faith into practice to be able to conquer anxiety.

Verses 29–30—Moreover, Jesus says, "Do not seek [the Greek says literally 'set your heart upon'] what you are to eat and what you are to drink, nor be worried." Focusing upon created things that perish rather than upon the imperishable love of God the Creator is not a believer's character but is the character of nonbelievers, "the nations of the world."

Verses 31–32—God's people are to keep on seeking His kingdom. They are to focus upon the areas of their life where God is continuing to rule, that is, providing for their daily needs as they journey on into His eternal kingdom. Jesus reminds them that the heavenly Father takes care of His "little flock." He is pleased to give them His kingdom, His active intervention in their lives for their welfare.

Verses 33–34—When believers discover they are "out of focus" and have an unhealthy attachment to this world's goods, they must do whatever it takes to bring their life into God's perspective. Christians are daily challenged to see the present in its perspective to what God will bring to His people. They need to focus on the true treasure given them: Jesus as their Savior. Jesus points out, "For where your treasure is, there will your heart be also." Those whose eyes are fixed upon the gracious Creator, who, as Jesus Christ, visited the earth to save it, will find that He guards their hearts and minds from the anxiety that comes from an attachment to the merely earthly and all that will eventually pass away (Philippians 4:6–9).

## 4 Creation's Apparent Contradictions

Many people have difficulty understanding or accepting the biblical testimony that, while God is in control of all things, each person is responsible for what is done within creation because humans are not puppets. This is an *antinomy*. An antinomy is a contradiction or inconsistency between two apparently reasonable principles or laws. People have difficulty when they face an antinomy because they often fall into dualistic reasoning. They assume that if an act is God's act then it cannot also be an act done voluntarily by a human. Or they reason that if a human person acts freely, then it is the person's act and not one also under God's governance.

But Scripture does not endorse such dualistic, either/or conclusions. Scripture does attribute a human being's ability to act to God's power. However, insofar as a particular act is attributed to a human being, that action of the human is judged by God to be either one that is good or evil. For example, one and the same act is said to be an act of self-hardening on Pharaoh's part as well as God's act of hardening Pharaoh's heart (compare Exodus 9:34 with 10:1).

According to Scripture, God does not worry that His purposes will be countermanded by society's sinful actions. Nor does God have to limit the freedom that all individuals have in earthly matters in order to preserve His lordship over them. They cannot blame what they do on "fate" or on God. The human conscience testifies to the reality that a man or woman is responsible before God for the evil directions of his or her actions (Romans 2:15).

There is both a directive will of God and a permissive will in the divine purpose. We see this in how the Son of God was treated on earth. Humans were blameworthy for crucifying the Lord of glory (Acts 2:23–24). Nevertheless, but as a permissive act of God, it still came under His total plan for how He would redeem the world.

God can and does work in all things for the good of those who love Him (Romans 8:28–29). Believers who confess their faith in our loving God know that in this life they still will experience the pain caused by sin. Christ's suffering and death brought about our salvation. So, too, does God use the suffering in our lives to conform us to Christ's image (Romans 5:1–4; 8:29). We are challenged to trust in God's good and wise governance of creation and its people as He moves us toward the glorious future of the new creation.

## 5 Responses to the Actions of God in Creation

Evil's continuing presence in the world is a challenge to a person's confidence that the Creator is wise, all-powerful, or even good. The attempt by some philosophers or skeptics to deal with the difficult question of evil and suffering being under God's control has been called *theodicy*, which means calling God to justify His relationship to suffering and evil. The Book of Job warns against it (Job 40:2, 8).

The reason a particular person undergoes a great suffering is found in the phrase (Deuteronomy 29:29) "secret things belong to the Lord our God." God reminds people, (Isaiah 55:8–9) "My thoughts are not your thoughts, neither are your ways, My ways."

The Scriptures do not present simple solutions for the perplexity that the existence of evil and suffering causes us. The Christian is neither an escapist nor a naive simpleton about the presence of much suffering and evil in this present world. Their existence is recorded many times in Scripture, beginning with Genesis 3. Furthermore, Jesus' crucifixion is ample testimony to the depth of evil and suffering. To onlookers, the suffering, dying Jesus appeared to affirm that evil had conquered good.

Those who attempt to live for God will not be exempt from suffering. The apostle Peter reminds suffering Christians, (1 Peter 4:12–13) "Beloved, do not be surprised at the fiery trial when it comes upon you to test you, as though something strange were happening to you. But rejoice insofar as you share Christ's sufferings, that you may also rejoice and be glad when His glory is revealed."

Scripture does not give a simple answer or explanation to evil's continuing existence in creation. Unlike other world religions and philosophies, Christianity does not explain the causes for all suffering. Instead, Christ suffered and thereby conquered it. For this reason, St. Paul told the sophisticated citizens of Corinth that he was determined not to use human wisdom to explain away evil. Instead, Paul focused upon the self-giving God in the crucified Christ (1 Corinthians 2:1–5). At that unique event in human history, God changed the history of all those people who are united to Christ through faith. For them, God has granted citizenship in God's sinless new creation yet to appear.

Somebody once said to Mrs. Albert Einstein, "Do you know all about your husband's theory of relativity?" Smiling, she replied, "No, but I know my husband, and I know he can be trusted." To speculate about why God still allows evil or suffering is useless. Their existence remains as challenges to Christians to plant their pain deeper into the faith that trusts in God's goodness, power, and wisdom. Following the examples of Job, who kept His focus upon God and His goodness (Job 42:1–6), and especially Jesus, who still trusted in His heavenly Father when the Father hid His face from Him as He hung on the cross as humanity's sin-bearer (Matthew 27:46), Christians, following Christ in all things, focus upon their heavenly Father's love. Thereby, they can be certain that He will give them victory on the other side of suffering and death. The resurrected Jesus is the living proof of this (Romans 8:39).

God, in Christ, has given proof that He can be trusted to make all things, even suffering, work for humanity's eternal good (Romans 8:28). He remains King of kings and Lord of lords despite the claim of others to be such (Revelation 19:16). The mightier the assault of wickedness, the greater God will reveal His ability to make His people victors.

### Conclusion

The triune God is the Almighty Creator and Gracious Giver, very much involved in preserving and guiding all that He has brought into existence. Because of their confidence of being victorious through Christ, Christians will praise Him evermore for all He created (Revelation 4:11). They will lift up their heads, hearts, and hands in the spirit of thanksgiving, saying to one another, (Psalm 118:1) "Give thanks to the Lord, for He is good; for His steadfast love endures forever!"

## Concluding Activities

Pray aloud: O most holy Trinity, great is Thy faithfulness; there is no shadow of turning with Thee. Thou changest not and Thy compassions fail not; as Thou hast been, Thou forever wilt be. Morning by morning new mercies we see. All we have needed Thy hand hath provided—so great is Thy faithfulness, Lord unto us! We give Thee thanks for pardon and a peace that endures; Thine own dear presence continues to cheer and to guide us. Strength for today and bright hope for tomorrow, blessings all ours, with ten thousand beside! Great is Thy faithfulness, Lord unto us! Amen. (Based on "Great Is Thy Faithfulness; *LSB* 809.)

Make any necessary announcements and distribute study leaflet 5.

# Son-Centered Creation

## Matthew 16:13–17; John 1:1–5; Colossians 1; John 5:17–29

*Preparing for the Session*

### Central Focus

*What* Jesus is and *who* Jesus is have been subjects of speculation and misrepresentation in the media. Is He just a man, though one of extraordinary religious sensitivity? What did He say about Himself? In this session, we will focus on Jesus Christ as the presence of God the Creator, come to earth to set free its inhabitants from their bondage to sin so that Judgment Day will be the day of entrance into the full life of a blessed eternity for those who trust His claims.

### Objectives

That participants, led by the Holy Spirit working through God's Word, will

1. confront the life-changing implications of knowing Jesus' unique identity;
2. be confident that Jesus is the victorious presence of the eternal Creator; and
3. turn only to Christ in trust for the way to a blessed eternal life.

**Note for the small-group leaders:** Lesson notes and other materials you will need begin on page 67.

### For the Lecture Leader

*Session Plan*

#### Worship

Begin the session with the hymn printed in the study leaflet. Accompaniments are available in denominational hymnals, such as *Lutheran Service Book* or *Lutheran Worship* (refer to hymnal index). (Note: Concordia Publishing House has available *The Concordia Organist*. All the initial worship hymns in the LifeLight courses are included in this resource. It's especially helpful for mission congregations and small parishes. See the list of study resources on page 7.) Follow with this prayer:

#### Prayer

Dear heavenly Father, grant us the gift of Your Holy Spirit that we may focus upon the significance of Your eternal Son as Your greatest gift to Creation. May Your Spirit enable us to tell others about Jesus so that they too may have the joy of eternal life He has brought to the world of sinners. Amen.

### Lecture Presentation

#### Introduction

When American astronauts first landed on the moon, it was rightly looked upon as a fantastic accomplishment. However, thousands of years before that moon landing, there was a historical event even more astonishing and life changing. It was when the Son of God arrived on earth to accomplish His redemptive work.

In the sixteenth century, Polish astronomer Nicolas Copernicus caused a revolution when he spoke of the sun, rather than the earth, as the center of the universe. Christians today know there is an even greater revolution they can initiate; one which is no less shocking to our culture. It is the Christian's privilege to announce that our planet earth is not only affected by the sun in the sky but also by Jesus Christ, the "sun of righteousness" (Malachi 4:2).

St. Paul praised the heavenly Father, (Ephesians 1:3) "who has blessed us in Christ with every spiritual blessing in the heavenly places, even as He chose us in Him before the foundation of the world." Jesus Christ is the mediator not only between God and humankind but also between creation and its fulfillment. The Book of Revelation speaks of Jesus as the "Alpha and the Omega," that is, the beginning of creation and its ultimate purpose and consummation (Revelation 1:8). To affirm that Jesus Christ is both the Creator and Redeemer is to view our galaxy as not only sun-centered but also gloriously "Son (spelled with an *o*) -centered!"

Creation and its redemption through Jesus Christ are part of the one great sweep of the divine love of the triune God that is personally creative, redemptive, and restorative. The Christian Church and its people are joyous to share the light of this good news to so many parts of the world that tragically still sits in spiritual darkness.

## 1 The Most Important Question (Matthew 16:13–17)

Verses 13–14—One day, Jesus took His disciples on a retreat to the upper region of ancient Palestine, into an area of the ruins of ancient pagan temples. While near Caesarea Philippi, Jesus asked His disciples what were the popular conceptions of their teacher. They replied that the opinions varied. Some people thought of Jesus as a great prophet, some thought of Him as one like Jeremiah, Elijah, or possibly the more recently martyred John the Baptizer, returned to life.

Verse 15—Then Jesus got personal and asked Peter directly, "But who do you say that I am?"

So what is Jesus? Is He partly god and partly man, a sort of demigod like the mythical Greek Hercules? Though Jesus is unquestionably famous, the bottom-line question of skeptics is "Isn't He just a man?" In 1971, British lyricist Tim Rice and musician Andrew Lloyd Webber produced the widely popular rock opera *Jesus Christ Superstar*. The opera character Mary Magdalene, who is in love with Jesus, sings, "I don't see why He moves me. He's a man. He's just a man. And I've had so many men before. In very many ways, He's just one more!"

Throughout its history, Christianity has confronted those who deny that Jesus is all that the name of God implies. The Arians (theological forerunners of today's Unitarians and Jehovah's Witnesses) mistook the Bible verses that refer to Jesus as the sinner's substitute (2 Corinthians 5:21) to be showing Jesus to be subordinate and inferior to Jehovah God. The Arians believed that Jesus was the highest being created by the One God. At the same time, however, the Arians said that because God honored Jesus by using Him to create the world, the Church is allowed to sing hymns praising Jesus. Likewise, Islam, though it speaks highly of Jesus as a moral man and God's greatest prophet, nevertheless considers it heresy worthy of death to anyone who says, "God has a Son."

Verse 16—Without realizing the full implications of his answer, Peter replied to Jesus' question of His identity, "You are the Christ [the Messiah, the specially appointed Deliverer sent by God], the Son of the living God."

Verse 17—Jesus' question to Peter is still crucial to each person's eternal salvation. A proper understanding of Jesus' uniqueness is the keystone in the arch of Christian theology, and the content of the Christian Church's good news to the world. Jesus is the center of His own message. Christianity is Christ. Unlike Moses, the Buddha, or Muhammad, who all claimed to give a message from God and pointed out the way that one is to live to be on the good side of God, Jesus said, (John 14:6) "*I am* [emphasis added] the way, and the truth, and the life." Acts 4:12 reminds us "There is salvation in no one else, for there is no other name under heaven given among men by which we must be saved."

Since the birth of Christianity, Christians have recognized that if Jesus were not all that God is, they would be guilty of idolatry by singing and worshiping one who is only a creature, despite His uniqueness (Exodus 20:3–4).

## 2 Jesus Is God, the Eternal Creative Word (John 1:1–5)

Verse 1—The evangelist John probes the mystery of Jesus' link between Creator and creation in the simple words "In the beginning was the Word, and the Word was with God, and the Word was God." The words "in the beginning" echoes the opening verse of Genesis. Just as the Hebrew Scriptures relate how God once brought all of creation into existence purely out of His own divine will, so too John reminds readers that the same God is again bringing forth a new creation through a special person simply called here "the Word" (the Greek word is *Logos*).

John 1:1 affirms that before time began, before the universe was created, there "was" the Word. A study of the Greek verb for "was" reveals that it is in the imperfect tense. This is the Greek tense that indicates a past continuous state and so asserts the eternal nature and timelessness of the Word.

In this opening verse, like a tight bud of a rose yet to reveal the fullness of it beauty, the truth of the distinction of persons within the Unity of the Godhead is starting to open. The evangelist John asserts that the eternal Word was "with God." The preposition "with" indicates both the equality of the persons of the Trinity and also that each person is distinct from the others. This is something that may not be obvious to a reader of the English text. The phrase "with God" is actually three words in the Greek text: *pros ton theon*. The Greek word *pros* can be translated as "toward" or "face-to-face." This indicates that the Word, though a distinct person within the Godhead, is equally God. Let me explain.

Middle Eastern and Oriental people were sensitive to ranking among people and the cultural significance of being face-to-face. If one was entertaining two guests of equal rank, they had to be seated on an equal level. If one was tall and the other short, the latter was seated upon pillows so that when he looked at the former their eyes met on an even line. Neither must look down upon or up to the other. Since they were equal in rank, they must see eye-to-eye, face-to-face. They were to be "toward" (*pros*) each other.

John further states explicitly that the Word is equally God with the Father: "And the Word was God," or literally translated, "God was the Word." This crucial statement is a point of controversy today among sects, especially the Jehovah's Witnesses, who deny that Jesus is fully divine.

Verse 2—The Word's equality with God is reaffirmed when John notes that the Word "was in the beginning with God." As the Father is the eternal Father, likewise the Son is the eternal Son.

Verse 3—Furthermore, "all things were made through" the Word. The Greek text literally says, "All things came into existence through Him"; that is, the creation of the universe came through Him. Thus He has the same attributes as God the Creator.

The last part of verse 3 can be translated "Without Him came into being not even one thing which has come into existence." The words "without Him" testify that the universe's origin and its continuing existence are solely due to the Word's power. The triune Godhead is sole Creator. No other intermediary beings are creators.

Verses 4–5—John goes on to say that in the Word "was life" (literally, "In Him always exists life"). The "life" that the Word has and brings to His followers is more than a simple biological existence. His gift of life is that wholeness that God intends for His creatures and that the Word's coming to earth makes possible as Jesus reconciles sinners to God.

## 3 Jesus Is the Preeminent Creator (Colossians 1)

The apostle Paul wrote his Letter to the Colossians because he received information from the Colossian pastor that members of his congregation were in danger of accepting an inadequate view of what Jesus Christ is. Colossae was geographically at the crossroads of the Eastern and Western Roman Empire. Christians in the territory were familiar with the uniting of different cultures, some of which were destructive to the scriptural truth about God.

Some agitators in Colossae were presenting a quasi-religious philosophical worldview known as *Gnosticism* (*gnosis* is Greek for "knowledge"). Paul calls their error a pernicious philosophy of "empty deceit" (2:8). The doctrinal agitators blended Gnosticism with elements of Judaism.

Because they viewed matter as being intrinsically evil, the Gnostics thought that the Supreme Being was unknowable and uninvolved in the material world. He could be worshiped only through a hierarchy of intermediary beings who acted as mediators between material beings and God, who was thought to be pure spirit.

Gnostic Christians viewed Christ simply as the highest "mediator" among many. To counteract the Gnostics errors, Paul paints a full-length of portrait of Jesus Christ that indicates He is preeminent over all supernatural beings and human religious activities. The apostle aggressively appeals to the Colossians to focus upon the fuller knowledge and wisdom that is hidden in Jesus Christ (Colossians 1:5, 9, 28; 2:3).

Verses 15–20—Paul seems to be quoting an early Christian hymn that extols Christ's deity and supremacy over creation. (V. 15a) "He is the image of the invisible God." While God made Adam and Eve *in* His image, Jesus Christ *is* that image in its most perfect sense. Like a mirror, Jesus perfectly reflects all that the essence of God is (John 1:18; 2 Corinthians 4:4; Hebrews 1:3).

Verse 15b—Jesus' supremacy over all created beings is that He is "the firstborn of all creation." To speak of Jesus as "firstborn" does not mean that He was the first creature to be made but that He has a unique, legal right of inheritance, like a Jewish eldest son (Deuteronomy 21:15–19). The firstborn in a Jewish family was accorded rights and privileges not shared by the other offspring. He was his father's representative and heir, and to him the management of the household was committed. Christ is His heavenly Father's representative and heir and has the management of the divine household (all creation) committed to Him. He is thus Lord over all God's creation.

Verses 16–17—Christ's superiority over creation is based on the fact that everything that is created owes its origin and continued existence to Him; indeed, "by Him all things were created. . . . He is before all things, and in Him all things hold together." He is "before" creation in the sense of rank and dignity. As Sustainer of all, He holds back chaos. He has no equal and no rival. He is the Lord of all, be it spiritual or material.

Because Colossians reveals that Christ is Lord over all parts of the Universe, Christians can appreciate science and space exploration while at the same time remembering that our galaxy is not only in a solar system but is also guided and controlled by the Son of God. He is its Creator (v. 16) and remains its Controller (v. 17).

Finally, Christians are to avoid a narrow goal in life that seeks merely material fulfillment. Only as one lives life in the light eternity does one's present material, bodily existence takes on true significance (Colossians 3:2).

## 4 As Creation's Judge, Jesus Is Due Divine Honor (John 5:17–20)

What is the purpose of people living in the world, and how will it all end for each of them? Jesus gave answers to these questions when He attended a festival at the Jerusalem temple.

The ancient world did not have a "day off" to rest from their manual or mental labors. Only Jews were privileged to have a Sabbath rest, which even their conquerors, the Romans, allowed them to celebrate.

However, as time went on, rabbis, in an effort to protect them from the wrath of God, built all kinds of rituals and laws around the Sabbath. In doing so, they turned the Sabbath into a burden, rather than a blessing. Jesus, as Lord of Sabbath, and the God who initiated the Sabbath rest, let His contemporaries know the Sabbath's original purpose. He often healed people—even those not in danger of dying without the healing—on the Sabbath. This was the case when He healed a cripple at a Jerusalem pool (John 5:2–9).

Verse 17—Jesus justified His Sabbath action on the grounds that He was simply following the example of "My Father." While Genesis 2:2 speaks of God's rest from all that He had made, nevertheless, God continues to work in the sense that He daily sustains and governs the world. Jesus, being one in "essence" with God the Father, sustained that part of creation present before Him—the disabled man that He healed.

Verse 18—Jesus' critics understood His words "My Father" as an expression of a very intimate relationship to God and an extraordinary claim to authority. According to His critics, Jesus had stepped out of a mortal man's proper relationship to one superior to Him. Jesus had become a rebellious son. Such a rebellious son was commonly referred to as having made himself "equal with God."

Verse 19—Standing firm in what He had said, Jesus even more forcefully asserted His equality with God the Father. Knowing that the Jews saw Him as a rebellious son of Abraham, Jesus rebutted the charge and stressed His perfect obedience to His Father's will. Jesus' Sabbath action is the very opposite of that of a rebellious son because everything He did was actually done in union with the Father's will. (Jesus says this repeatedly: John 4:34; 5:30; 8:28; 12:50; 15:10). As divine persons, the Father and the Son are not only equal in divine dignity but also in affection, purpose, and will.

Verse 20a—The relationship of God the Father to the Son is one of such close love that the Father shows to the Son all of His work. Thus, any follower of Jesus can be confident that in His words the heavenly Father's will is being perfectly revealed. (See also John 14:7–10). To know Christ is to know God.

Verse 20b—Jesus' Sabbath healing of the poolside cripple scandalized Jesus' critics. They then received an even greater shock in what He claimed to have the power to do.

## 5 Jesus, the Judge of All Humanity, Is the Source of Resurrection Life (John 5:21–29)

Verse 21—Jewish rabbis were convinced that only God has the power to resurrect the dead. Jesus shocked them by asserting that He is not simply God's instrument, as Elijah and Elisha had been, to raise the dead. Jesus asserted that His authority is that of God Himself, who "gives life to whom He will." However, in the Gospel of John, the word "life" refers to more than just physical life (John 11:25–26); it refers to the spiritual life of eternity with God as well.

Verses 22–24—The controversy among the Jerusalem critics of Jesus was not really about His working on the Sabbath but about who and what He claimed to be. Thus Jesus went on to describe the self-condemnation His critics were inflicting upon themselves by refusing to accept the witness of His work and words that bear testimony to His unique identity.

Verse 22—Jesus told His critics that His Father is not directly judging any person but has committed such judgment to the Son. Here, Jesus makes another claim of divinity, that He does the work of final judgment. Jesus claims that He will not only resurrect all people on the last day of the present creation but on that day He will also be their Judge.

Verse 23—The purpose of the heavenly Father having the Son publicly execute the final judgment is to show humanity the honor the Son of God possesses as the Son of Man. Jesus has asserted His equality with God (v. 18). Now, because of this equality, Jesus can say "that all may honor the Son, *just as* [emphasis added] they honor the Father. Whoever does not honor the Son does not honor the Father who sent Him." Possessing divine attributes and doing divine works, Jesus is to be given divine honor and glory. No other world religious leader can say that!

Verse 24—After this word of warning, Jesus again invited them to salvation. He assured them that if they would hear and believe in Him as the Sent-One of the Father, then they would be "passed from death to life."

Verses 25–29—Jesus' Jerusalem critics were shocked by His "work" of healing the paralytic at the Bethsaida pool, but He urged them to hold their amazement in check. He informed them (v. 25) that "an hour is coming." This was speaking of the day of final public judgment of all people, when they will see what happens to those who have not taken Him seriously (v. 28). Verse 29 says that a blessed "life" will be given to "those who have done good." But to "those who have done evil [will go] to the resurrection of judgment (condemnation)." "Those who have done good" are people who are connected to Him, and, therefore, those whom the heavenly Father will pronounce good and will bless with eternal life (see John 3:21; Hebrews 11:6).

## Conclusion

A chasm exists between the Holy Creator and the fallen creation, and only the Creator can bridge it. The note of victory in the Gospel is that, in the life and ministry of Jesus, God did close the gap. How can we sinners be sure that Christ' work reconciles us to God? Paul says we have this assurance because of who Christ is: the image of the invisible God, the Creator, and the one who is preeminent over all things.

"What else would you look to for assurance? To an angel? To yourself? No, look to God Himself in Christ" (*The Lutheran Study Bible,* St. Louis, Concordia, 2009, p. 2044). Though this unique person, Jesus of Nazareth, is an intrinsic part of earth's history, He comes to the earth as one who had existence before the earth and all planets in the universe came to be. History is primarily "His story" because He is history's Lord.

## Concluding Activities

Pray aloud: Dear heavenly Father, we thank and praise You for Your love that did not turn away from Your creation but so loved our fallen world that you sent Your only-begotten Son to set it free from its bondage to sin. We look to no other wisdom or ritual as the path upon we walk into a blessed eternity but Christ alone. He is preeminent in our heart because He is the living Lord God, Creator, in whom our redemption is secure and our bodily resurrection to glory certain. Because of Him, we are confident enough to call You our heavenly Father. Amen.

Make any necessary announcements and distribute study leaflet 6.

# His Life: My Life

## John 1:14; Romans 5:12–17

*Preparing for the Session*

## Central Focus

Non-Christian world religions stress that it is humans who must do something to placate an angry, hidden god. The devout will send their sons to die for the deity, sacrifice their virgins, or even tear out their own heart to make the god happy. The unique testimony of Christianity is that humans do not have to reach up to the deity or try to buy Him off with sacrifices. The wondrous Christian message is that God came down to be fully human among us, to experience all the negatives of our existence, and to die a most shameful death for us. God did this because of His love for creation and its crown, human beings. By entering fully into human life, and by living the will of God on earth as it is in heaven, the Son of God has obtained for us eternal blessings.

## Objectives

That participants, led by the Holy Spirit working through God's Word, will

1. rejoice that God's love for creation was proven in His full involvement in all the difficult stages of human life to sanctify it by voluntarily dying in humanity's place to bring it eternal benefits;

2. find comfort in their struggle with sin, knowing that Jesus remains forever their heavenly intercessor; and

3. walk through life with a vision of Christ's victory on their behalf that enables them to live like Him.

**Note for the small-group leaders:** Lesson notes and other materials you will need begin on page 69.

## For the Lecture Leader

*Session Plan*

### Worship

Begin the session with the hymn printed in the study leaflet. Accompaniments are available in denominational hymnals, such as *Lutheran Service Book* or *Lutheran Worship* (refer to hymnal index). (Note: Concordia Publishing House has available *The Concordia Organist*. All the initial worship hymns in the LifeLight courses are included in this resource. It's especially helpful for mission congregations and small parishes. See the list of study resources on page 7.) Follow with this prayer:

### Prayer

Dear heavenly Father, we are so prone to fear and loneliness. We forget that You entered fully into our humanity through Your Son, Jesus Christ, so that we can know You understood our need to be comforted. May Your Holy Spirit help us keep our focus upon Christ, who shows us what humanity was created to be and who has come among us to be the "in-the-flesh" source of inner peace and the preview of a blessed future for each of our lives.

## Lecture Presentation

### Introduction

Little four-year old Julia was having trouble sleeping. It was thundering and lightning outside, and the outline of the swaying tree on the window shade was creating scary figures. At one particularly loud thunderclap, Julia cried out, "Daddy! Daddy, I'm scared!" Her father called back, "Don't be afraid, dear; your loving God is with you!" There were a few moments of silence, then another thunderclap. "Daddy! Daddy! Come here. Come here. Please!" Her father got up, rushed into her room, and put his arms around her.

"Are you okay now, my dear Julia?" he asked. She replied, "Yes, Daddy, yes. I just needed love with some skin on it!" Don't even adults, all of us, want such personal love?

God the Creator knows our physical, social, and—above all—spiritual needs, and so He got involved in them. "The Word became flesh and dwelt among us" is the astonishing, wonderful announcement we needed to hear from God's Word (John 1:14).

## 1 God Puts "Skin" On (John 1:14)

With words that shocked those holding the ancient Jewish and Greek ideas of God, the evangelist John wrote, "The Word became flesh." The apostle Paul also wrote that in Jesus of Nazareth "the whole fullness of deity dwells bodily (Colossians 2:9).

God the Creator does not despise the physical side of creation. At a certain moment in history, the Second Person within the Godhead united His personhood to a complete human nature. Becoming Jesus of Nazareth, God took the initiative to use creation for a redemptive purpose. Luke 1:35 records that the angel Gabriel informed the Virgin Mary that the Holy Spirit, in a miraculous manner, would generate the human nature of the Second Person of the divine Trinity from the substance of her body. As the first Adam came directly from the hand of God through the substance of the earth, so God again created a new man through the substance of Mary's body. Luke's genealogy of Jesus describes Him as the "son of Adam, the son of God" (3:38). Thus, Jesus is referred to as the "Second Adam" (see Romans 5:17).

At the first Christmas, God brought to earth a "new Adam" who overcame sin's ravages upon creation that the Adam of the Garden of Eden brought to us. Additionally, Jesus' conception in a virgin's body reminds us that salvation is solely through God's initiative. All sinners can do is receive it in wonder and acknowledge that God is to be praised, as did Mary and Joseph.

When the Son of God came to earth, He became fully human without ceasing to be God. From the cradle to the grave, Jesus acted as the obedient new Adam. Luke 2:21–24 describes how Jesus was circumcised and then later presented in the temple in the same way as every baby boy who was dedicated to God.

Luke 2:50 records that Jesus "was submissive to" his earthly parents. A few verses later, Luke 2:52 shows the normality of Jesus' life and its difficulties, especially during the adolescent years. The Greek text says, literally, that Jesus "chopped His way forward" ("increased") through the challenges of those years in order to grow "in wisdom and in stature."

Scripture records nothing about Jesus' private life for the next eighteen years in the home of Mary and Joseph. About 80 to 90 percent of Jesus' visible presence on earth was spent in the Galilean village of Nazareth, in obscurity among his earthly family. Jesus' work of being humanity's redeemer during those obscure years in Nazareth was accomplished not by being different from humanity but by being the same with a holy difference. He did not desire to have fame and glory but to serve His earthly family and the villagers of Nazareth.

Matthew 13:55 describes Him as a skilled laborer (Greek: *Tekton*, a worker in stone, wood, leather). Jesus earned his living by hard work. Hebrews 2:16–18 assures us that Jesus personally knew how exhausting life on earth is for us humans as we endure the difficulty of earning a livelihood.

Acting as the head of a new humanity and as our representative, Jesus faced temptations by Satan, mankind's spiritual enemy (Luke 4:1–4). During the forty-day stay in the Judean wilderness, Satan approached Jesus in the same way he had approached Adam and Eve. Satan tested Jesus to see if Jesus would seek a quick path to glory or follow the world's vision of success, rather than suffering for obeying God's vision. But according to Luke 4:4, 8, 12, Jesus defeated those temptations with the same sword God puts in our hands: Scripture.

Moreover, Jesus knows personally how difficult human relationships can be. Mark 6:1–5 records that Jesus' hometown people misunderstood Him. In their stubborn presumptuousness, they thought they knew Him (including those among family members), but they didn't. Jesus could do nothing for them because they created a barrier of unbelief. All He could do was "marvel . . . because of their unbelief."

Jesus personally knew sorrow and the reality of death. He became angry and then wept at the death of His friend Lazarus (John 11:33–35).

Because the Son of God, the Creator, took unto Himself a full humanity, whatever Jesus does is relevant to *our* humanity. The Son of God, incarnate as Jesus, has shown us that even with our bodies (and not just with our spirits), we have been created to serve and glorify God (Romans 12:1–2).

## 2 The Creator Redeems Humanity on a Wooden Cross (Romans 5:12–17)

Verse 12—All human beings born through natural reproduction possess Adam and Eve's same spiritual condemnation and guilt and proclivity toward sin. That's bad news, and it's a fact that ancient Judaism also acknowledged. The ancient Jews believed that one person could "stand in for" other people so completely that what happened to the stand-in actually happened to the people also. It did not happen to him instead of them; his experience *was* their experience.

Verse 14—Now comes the good news connected to a "second Adam," Jesus. At His Baptism, Jesus identified

Himself so completely with sinners that John the Baptizer was hesitant to baptize Him (Matthew 3:14). But Jesus said, (Matthew 3:15) "Let it be so now, for thus it is fitting for us to fulfill all righteousness."

Verse 17—Immediately after Jesus' Baptism, Satan recognized that Jesus was standing in the place of humanity. So Satan confronted Jesus with the same type of temptation Adam and Eve faced in the Garden of Eden. Their sin was to grasp at power and not trust in the heavenly Father's timetable and methods for one's life. Jesus, however, did not grasp at power but trusted in His heavenly Father's will. Jesus would walk only in the way of His Father's will, no matter how difficult.

Jesus' obedient walk eventually led to His suffering on the cross. On Good Friday, Jesus took every sinner with Him onto the cross and there put to death in His tomb the old era of the first Adam.

A pastor once told a story about a young Christian girl who finally had an inclination of what Jesus did to bring about her forgiveness of sin. She had been frightened by an angry bee and, unable to chase it away, she ran to her mother and hid behind her. As the mother put her arms around her little daughter to protect her, the bee settled upon the mother's arm and stung her deeply. The mother then assured her little daughter that she was perfectly safe. The bee could not sting twice.

In a greater way, Jesus put His arms around all sinners and took the sting of sin upon Himself. He provides safety for all who flee to His protecting arms. This good news for each of us is found in 1 Corinthians 15:56–57: "The sting of death is sin, and the power of sin is the law. But thanks be to God, who gives us the victory through our Lord Jesus Christ." The apostle Paul tells us more about this "great exchange" in 2 Corinthians 5:21: "For our sake, He [God] made Him [Jesus Christ] to be sin who knew no sin, so that in Him we might become the righteousness of God." The apostle Peter also speaks about this "great exchange" when he writes, (1 Peter 3:18) "For Christ also suffered once for sins, the righteous for the unrighteous, that He might bring us to God."

To the repentant thief on the cross, Jesus said, (Luke 23:43) "Truly I say to you, today you will be with Me in Paradise." In Greek, the word for *paradise* also means "garden." A tree was connected with Adam and Eve's removal from Eden, but a tree made into a cross, upon which Jesus Christ, the Second Adam, was crucified, brought back all of the First Adam's descendants (you and me) into God's eternal Eden (Galatians 3:13–14).

## 3 Jesus' Bodily Resurrection Previews Creation's Restoration

Jesus had a real life, and His death was so real that He was buried (John 19:40–42). But that is not the end of His story. The Ancient Church's greeting was a dramatic reminder of this: "He is risen!" Christian hearers would then respond, "He is risen indeed!"

St. Peter's words in Acts 2:24 testify that without the reality of Jesus' bodily resurrection, Christianity would not exist, for it would lack the message of a victorious hope that the world in bondage to sin, suffering, and death needs. Peter said this of Jesus: "God raised Him up, loosing the pangs of death, because it was not possible for Him to be held by it."

Without the assurance that Jesus is very much alive and among His followers still, Christianity would have remained only a small, revolutionary movement led by a moral but deluded teacher who died like everyone else. Moreover, if Jesus' body was still a corpse in a tomb, then His cross, the central symbol of Christianity, would be a sign of defeat rather than a sign testimony to heaven's victory.

But Jesus *is* alive. Christians do not worship a dead rabbi but the living Lord! On Easter morning, an angel said to the women visitors to Jesus' tomb that Jesus was not found among the dead (Luke 24:5–6). The substance of the same body that had suffered the death on the cross was given new life on the third day after Jesus' crucifixion. On Easter evening, Jesus told His startled followers, "See My hands and My feet, that it is I Myself" (Luke 24:39).

However, the resurrected Jesus is more than a resuscitated corpse. Jesus' risen body is the kind that "suits" the eternal state of existence. It is a type of body not limited by earth's time and space. All Christians will be given such a glorious body when the present creation ends (Philippians 3:21; 1 Corinthians 15:43). Therefore, the resurrected Jesus, standing before His assembled disciples, could give them the encouraging words, (Matthew 28:20) "I am with you always." He created an exit out of the grave, and death did not defeat Him.

The resurrected Jesus said, (Matthew 28:18) "All authority in heaven and on earth has been given to Me." The Jesus we meet in Revelation 1:17–18 says this: "Fear not, I am the first and the last, and the living one. I died, and behold I am alive forevermore, and I have the keys of Death and Hades." Jesus' resurrection demonstrates that only He is Lord over life and death.

For Jesus' followers, His resurrection is like a receipt from heaven's bank that certifies that sin now has no claim on them. Here is an illustration: When a prisoner is reintroduced into society, the release is a statement that the debt to society has been paid. Our heavenly Father accepted Jesus' perfect life and death as the substitute payment for our debt to God as sinners. St. Paul recognized this glorious fact when he wrote, (1 Corinthians 15:17) "If Christ has not been raised, your faith is futile and you are still in your sins." But Paul could announce to us this good news that Jesus was (Romans 4:25) "delivered up [to death] for our trespasses and raised for [because of] our justification."

Moreover, Jesus' bodily resurrection previews that of His followers. Christians can be certain about a glorious life beyond the grave because they have seen this in Jesus' bodily resurrection. Second Corinthians 5:17 announces, "Therefore, if anyone is in Christ, he is a new creation. The old has passed away; behold, the new has come."

Jesus' bodily resurrection gives Christians a positive message to proclaim to a world racked by sin and death. Death does not have the last word—the Son of the living God does! Therefore, He promises us, (John 14:19) "Because I live, you also will live." The Holy Spirit, in our Baptism, united us to the living Christ so that now we only "rent" our graves.

## 4 Earth's Dust Now Sits on Heaven's Throne

For forty days after leaving His tomb, Jesus demonstrated before many witnesses that He was indeed alive (Acts 1:3). He also talked to them about their tasks as instruments of God's rule on earth (Matthew 28:18–20).

Then Jesus visibly and dramatically departed from earth to signal a new way that He would be working among Christians (Luke 24:51; Acts 1:9 –11).

Jesus' visible ascension occurred outside Jerusalem, near Bethany. To assure His overly earth-minded disciples that His departure would actually be positive for them, Jesus first lifted up His hands and blessed them (Luke 24:50).

The ascension was for the benefit of onlookers, and it served to remind them of the present nature of Jesus' kingdom. Contrary to their wishes, His *visible* kingdom would not be established until His dramatic second coming (Acts 1:11b). Jesus did not give His followers a timetable regarding when that return would be. Rather, He has given them an important task (and it is a privilege to carry it out). He commanded them (and us) to perform tasks of teaching and baptizing, with His authority enabling that ministry, until His visible return to end the present-era of our universe (Matthew 28:19).

Jesus' visible withdrawal from His first-century followers was traumatic for them. Nevertheless, they needed it to see that they are now expected to be His "hands" and "feet," to actively teach and preach on His behalf.

Though Jesus would no longer be visible to His earthly followers, He would, nevertheless, remain very close to them. He would be enabling them through the ministry of the Holy Spirit. He promised, (John 16:7) "Nevertheless, I tell you the truth: it is to your advantage that I go away, for if I do not go away, the Helper will not come to you. But if I go, I will send Him to you." Paul writes about Jesus: (Ephesians 4:8, 11–12) "When He ascended on high He led a host of captives, and He gave gifts to men. . . . And He gave the apostles, the prophets, the evangelists, the shepherds and teachers, to equip the saints for the work of ministry, for building up the body of Christ."

Finally, for each of us today, Jesus' earthly followers, His bodily ascension assures us that He is keeping His promise about our future. He truly is preparing an eternal place for us in the glory of His heavenly Father. Prior to His crucifixion and resurrection, Jesus said, (John 14:2) "In My Father's house are many rooms. If it were not so, would I have told you that I go to prepare a place for you?"

Because of Jesus Christ, those who trust in Him to take care of their greatest treasure—life itself—can be confident that their life is like a ship that will bring them to the safe port of a blessed eternity. Playing upon the word *ship*, we can say that discipleship with Jesus will safely dock us in the place of fellowship with all of Christ's resurrected believers in heaven's eternity.

## 5 Jesus' Power at the Father's Right Hand

Late on the night before His crucifixion, Jesus told the accusing temple high priest, (Matthew 26:64) "From now on you will see the Son of Man seated at the right hand of Power and coming on the clouds of heaven." But what did Jesus mean? God does not literally have a physical right hand! The "right hand of God" is an expression that uses something earthly to compare it with something that is not material. Such figurative speech requires the hearer to seek the point of comparison. Christ's human nature, because of its eternal union to His divine nature, is at last and forever free from all limitations of time and space. To say Jesus ascended to the right hand of God is a human way to express the truth that Jesus now exercises His heavenly power. The psalmist wrote, (Psalm 20:6) "Now I know that the Lord saves His anointed; He will answer Him from His holy heaven with the saving might of His right hand." Moses offers his praise to God: (Exodus 15:6) "Your right hand, O Lord, glorious in power . . . shatters the enemy."

Additionally, it is a comforting reminder to us Christians that we have a continuous intercessor, a heavenly High Priest. Believers have an "in" in the throne room of the heavenly Father. In Ephesians 1:20, Paul comforts the Church with the good news that God the Father set His Son at His right hand as His earthly followers' representative and intercessor.

Whenever we fall into sin and Satan accuses us before God, demanding that we be damned like he is, Jesus intercedes for us on the basis of His accomplished redemption. Paul writes, (Romans 8:34) "Who is to condemn [us]? Christ Jesus is the one who died—more than that, who was raised—who is at the right hand of God, who indeed is interceding for us." He throws out of heaven Satan's accusations against us believers. For this reason, the evangelist John writes, (1 John 2:1) "If anyone does sin, we have an advocate with the Father, Jesus Christ the righteous."

Finally, knowing that Jesus is God's "right-hand man" is an encouragement for us to live our lives in light of Christ's continuing gifts to us. Paul motivated the Colossian Christians to live a more spiritual life by telling them, (Colossians 3:1) "If then you have been raised with Christ, seek the things that are above, where Christ is, seated at the right hand of God."

Because Jesus, divine love "with skin," has united us to Himself through the Holy Spirit received in Baptism, we are truly enabled to obtain daily His victory. God's "right-hand man" has made His life of victory that of our life too.

### Conclusion

Jesus in not only fully God but He is also fully human. St. Paul calls this a "mystery." (A "problem" is solvable, but a "mystery" remains just that.) The apostle writes, (1 Timothy 3:16) "Great indeed, we confess, is the mystery of godliness: He was manifested in the flesh, vindicated by the Spirit, seen by angels, proclaimed among the nations, believed on in the world, taken up in glory."

In His prayer to His Father, Jesus said this about us, His earthly followers: (John 17:22) "The glory that You have given Me I have given to them, that they may be one even as We are one." Because Jesus is God, the Creator who entered into earthly time and space to become fully human without ceasing to be God, those who are connected to Him through faith and adopted by the Holy Spirit into the family of the triune God, can say, "His life is my life." And we joyfully exclaim with St. Paul, (Philippians 1:21) "For me to live is Christ, and to die is gain."

## Concluding Activities

Pray aloud: We thank You, dear heavenly Father, that You sent Your only-begotten Son to live among us and for us. He was perfectly obedient to You, even to death upon the cross. We praise Your holy name and rejoice that in Your Son's sacrificial death, all our sins are forgiven and a blessed bodily resurrection is guaranteed in our future. We turn to Him daily as our intercessor as we wage war against the sins that still oppress us. Yet we live our lives confident of victory because we know that the Holy Spirit's baptismal work upon us has made Christ's life our victorious life as well. Amen.

Make any necessary announcements and distribute study leaflet 7.

# Heavenly Blessings through Earthly Elements

## Selected Passages

*Preparing for the Session*

### Central Focus

God in Christ is involved at times in amazingly direct ways in human life, using what He Himself created, in order to preserve, nurture, and bring abundant joy. Christians are called to activate their faith connection to the Christ of creation in order to face crises without fear but with confidence.

### Objectives

That participants, led by the Holy Spirit working through God's Word, will

1. find joy in how Jesus Christ uses His power for the benefit of the needy;
2. have confidence in the power of Christ to meet human need today; and
3. appreciate the Holy Spirit's use of special rites of water, bread, and wine as His vehicles of continual and unique divine blessing.

**Note for the small-group leaders:** Lesson notes and other materials you will need begin on page 72.

### For the Lecture Leader

*Session Plan*

#### Worship

Begin the session with the hymn printed in the study leaflet. Accompaniments are available in denominational hymnals, such as *Lutheran Service Book* or *Lutheran Worship* (refer to hymnal index). (Note: Concordia Publishing House has available *The Concordia Organist*. All the initial worship hymns in the LifeLight courses are included in this resource. It's especially helpful for mission congregations and small parishes. See the list of study resources on page 7.) Follow with this prayer:

#### Prayer

Dear heavenly Father, like Israel of old, and like Jesus' disciples, we are prone to forget that You have connected us to the power of Your Son through Baptism and now give us the comforting hug of His body and blood in the Lord's Supper. Give us Your Holy Spirit through the Sacred Scriptures that He will motivate us to exercise Your gift of faith in a way that exhibits to others the victorious life of your children. Amen.

### Lecture Presentation

#### Introduction

What Jesus is, is unique. He is of both heaven and earth. He stated that if you do not believe what He said, you should at least take a closer look at what He did (John 10:25, 38). Peter, speaking to a crowd said, (Acts 2:22) "Men of Israel, hear these words: Jesus of Nazareth, a man attested to you by God with mighty works and wonders and signs that God did through Him in your midst, as you yourselves know."

Jesus did "miracles," that is, striking or unusual workings of God that are not explainable to the onlooker on the basis of the usual patterns of nature. Because miracles are rare, people recognized that they are to be evaluated only on the basis of some direct power from the supernatural. As unusual actions of God, miracles are not open to human explanation, but humans are to receive them with awe, wonder, and praise.

#### 1 The Weight of Joy at a Wedding (John 2:1–11)

Jesus attended banquets and ate with friends and foe alike. Some people wondered why Jesus wasn't more selective, more standoffish, like a lot of other "holy men" who typically kept to themselves in the desert or monastery. Jesus enjoyed people and parties! In fact, His first miracle was during a village wedding at Cana. This miracle has significance beyond Jesus' providing the best wine. But what is it? The evangelist John gives us clues when he writes, (John 2:11) "This, the first of His signs, Jesus did at Cana in Galilee, and manifested His glory. And His disciples believed in Him."

John calls Jesus' Cana miracle a "sign" because it points beyond itself to something special about the doer of the marvelous action. A close look at the details connected with this "sign-miracle" at Cana reveals marvelous truths regarding Jesus' unique nature and mission in relationship to the created world and to us.

Jesus' first wondrous deed has significance because it took place at a wedding, where family units are created. An ancient Jewish wedding didn't involve just the immediate family, but the whole village, and they celebrated for at least a week. Because of the sense of joy and community of such weddings, Isaiah uses the picture of a wedding feast to symbolize the days of happiness and abundance God's deliverer, the Messiah, would bring to His people (see 25:6–8; 62:4–5). Jesus once referred to Himself and His disciples as a wedding group (Mark 2:19–20). In one of His parables, Jesus made use of a marriage banquet as an analogy of the messianic age (Matthew 22:2). John the Baptizer referred to Jesus as the Church's Bridegroom (John 3:29). Additionally, Revelation 21:9 speaks of the Church as the Bride of the Lamb, Christ.

Adding impact to the miraculous sign from Jesus is His creation of a lot of wine from water. In many Old Testament passages, such as Amos 9:13–14, wine in abundance signifies the overflowing prosperity and joyous life that the Messiah's coming would bring to our planet. Jesus later said, (John 10:10) "I came that they may have life and have it abundantly."

At this Cana marriage, Jesus exhibited His "glory" (John 2:11). The Greek word for *glory* has the sense of "weight." The miracle at Cana was a sign that the weight of God's presence was in Jesus. Under the Old Covenant, God worked certain "signs" that were considered miraculous and testified to His gracious presence among His people. Jesus is the same God but under the New Covenant. Only the Creator can transform one substance (water) into another (wine); Jesus proved that He possesses the power of the Creator.

Additionally at the wedding, Jesus overcame what to some people may seem to be an insignificant need—the lack of wine at a large celebration. Yet, Jesus' action indicates that, in Jesus, His followers meet God as He who is willing and able to provide for all human need, no matter how insignificant that need may be (Romans 8:31–32; James 1:17). Jesus is the presence of the gracious Creator, who is limitless in His willingness and ability to give a life of abundant joy.

## 2 Stirring Up Faith in the Middle of a Storm (Matthew 8:23–27; Luke 8:22–25; Mark 4:35–41)

Throughout His ministry on earth, Jesus was recognized by common people as someone who was there for their needs, and so they constantly surrounded Him. After one particularly exhausting day, "when Jesus saw a crowd around Him" (Matthew 8:18), He decided to leave Capernaum, His headquarters along the Sea of Galilee, and cross to the other side, to a predominately non-Jewish region. Jesus decided to also take His disciples with Him.

The sailing of Jesus and His crew was peaceful at first. Being exhausted, Jesus fell asleep. But things were about to change dramatically. Mountains surround the Sea of Galilee on almost all sides. Especially at night, storms can quickly develop. Warm air from around the lake rises, but cool air rushes down from the mountains to take its place, often creating a violent wind. Such a sudden violent atmospheric change descended upon Jesus and His disciples, and it whipped up the waves so much that the group's boat began to fill with water and put them "in danger" (Luke 8:23b).

Nevertheless, as the storm raged, Jesus continued to sleep calmly on the boat's high afterdeck (Mark 4:38a), away from the splashing waves. Jesus slept through the storm because of His trust in His heavenly Father's care for Him in all circumstances. While Jesus remained as calm as the lake had previously been, the disciples' emotions were churning. These experienced fishermen knew their craft was in danger of sinking. So they rushed over to Jesus to wake Him up, crying out to Him their fear of death (Luke 8:24). They also expressed their annoyance with Him that He could sleep so peacefully in this situation. After the wedding-of-Cana miracle, they knew Jesus had some unusual abilities. So why wasn't He using them? They confronted Him with the question of whether He cared about them (Mark 4:38b).

Now awake, Jesus did not leave the disciples in their panic. It is noteworthy that Jesus did not pray that God calm the storm. He didn't need to. Jesus has all the authority of God the Creator (Colossians 2:9). Jesus directly calmed the waves with a word of rebuke, (Mark 4:39) "Peace! Be still!" (Literally, "be muzzled.") Jesus' order is similar to what He said when He performed an exorcism (Mark 1:25). Perhaps the violent storm had demonic forces behind it. In Scripture, the chaos of the sea was a traditional image for evil forces that only God can control (Psalm 65:7). Jesus is God, and now with a command, He wields His godly power on behalf of His loved ones. Jesus is the incarnation of the caring God who is involved continually in creation!

But Jesus also had to chide the disciples. (Mark 4:40) "Why are you so afraid? Have you still no faith?" These questions emphasize that often a Christian's faith has as its opposite not doubt, but unwarranted fear.

The disciples' problem was not that they lacked faith but that their faith was forgetful under pressure. The disciples were not exercising their faith in Christ in that crisis. What Jesus was doing to them on that stormy lake was an object lesson on the importance of active believing. Jesus acknowledges the difficulty faith faces in overcoming human fear in the presence of the awesome power of creation.

Jesus' miracle filled the disciples with a reverent fear in the face of divine power at work so closely in front of them. They ask, (Mark 4:41b) "Who then is this, that even the wind and the sea obey Him?" This miracle revealed Jesus as the Lord of any of the chaotic elements within creation that demonic angels may hurl at God's people to cause them fear.

Just as believers in Bible-times prayed to God for deliverance from perils of the sea, so we today can confidently turn to Jesus. He is the same God whom the psalmist confidently prayed to with the words, (Psalm 89:8–9) "O Lord God of hosts [armies of angels], who is mighty as You are, O Lord, with Your faithfulness all around You? You rule the raging of the sea; when its waves rise, You still them."

## 3 Want Not; Waste Not! (Mark 6:30–44; Luke 9:10–17; John 6:1–14)

Jesus and the Twelve, upon crossing over the lake, reached a deserted area. Nevertheless, the persistent crowds eventually located them, because people were attracted to Jesus' miracles (John 6:2). Some of them were probably Jewish nationalists who hoped Jesus would lead a revolt to expel the Roman conquerors. At that time, it was assumed that it would be during a Passover season that the Messiah would make His sudden appearance.

Although the people were attracted to Him for the wrong reasons, Jesus did not let this Passover crowd go away without speaking to them about God's activity (that is, "the kingdom of God"; Luke 9:11) that was present in what He was doing.

When evening came, the disciples were aware that the crowd needed to be fed. But they were in an area without shops to purchase food. Even if there were such shops, they would have been closed, since it was so late (Mark 6:35). The disciples' only solution was to ask Jesus to dismiss these hungry people so that they could go elsewhere to be taken care of (Luke 9:12). The disciples still did not exhibit Jesus' total self-giving on behalf of the needs of others.

Jesus asked Philip, (John 6:5) "Where are we to buy bread, so that these people may eat?" Jesus' question certainly pointed out their inability to do so. But Jesus' question also prepared them to see that Jesus can answer the prayer He had taught them, "Gives us this day our daily bread," because He does the will of God on earth as it is in heaven.

Moreover, when the disciples heard Jesus say, (Mark 6:37) "You give them something to eat," they felt as if they were facing an impossible task. Yet, no task is ever impossible for Christ. So no Christian today can rightfully plead lack of resources to meet human need when Jesus is trusted.

Still thinking only in earthly concepts, the disciples responded to Jesus' instruction in a purely monetary way. They reminded Him that they did not have enough money to feed so large a crowd. However, Andrew had located a boy with five barley loaves and two small fish. Yet Andrew, like Philip and the others, knew that they could not feed so many with such small provisions (John 6:9b).

In the midst of human helplessness, Jesus stepped in and took charge. Representing the God of order, Jesus told the disciples to arrange the crowd into "groups of about fifty each" (Luke 9:14). This is similar to what Moses did in Exodus 18:25. Jesus, as the Good Shepherd, had them sit down upon the "green" pasture (Mark 6:39) to be fed by Him.

Reminding humanity that God takes care of their bodily needs, Jesus took the bread and fishes into His hands and "looked up to heaven." As He did so, He offered His prayer of thanksgiving to God for the food (and for what He would do with and through the food).

After Jesus prayed His thanksgiving to God, He instructed the disciples to distribute to the needy what little portion they had given Him and which He wanted them to share with others. Soon the crowd recognized that something out of the ordinary was happening. What had come from Jesus' hands was enough for over five thousand to eat until they were all completely satisfied.

At that moment, the people recognized the miraculous feeding to be a sign (John 6:14a) that Moses' prophecy had now been fulfilled. Moses had foretold, according to Deuteronomy 18:15, 18, of the greater Prophet who would one day arrive in the midst of His people to feed them. Hence, this Passover crowd was buzzing with excitement that Jesus was that greater-than-Moses Prophet (John 6:14b). Indeed, Jesus is much more than a prophet. Jesus is God, the Savior of creation, who has come to lead people not from political oppression but from sin's corrupting bondage.

## 4 Walking in Faith, Not Afraid (Matthew 14:22–33; Mark 6:45–52; John 6:16–21)

After miraculously feeding the crowd of five thousand, Jesus directed the disciples to leave the area by boat. By the time the Twelve set out across the Sea of Tiberias (Galilee), it was quite late. But obediently, they were carrying out Jesus' wishes. For a time, they were separated from Jesus.

About midway in their journey across the lake, the disciples' boat was so buffeted by waves (Matthew 14:24) that they had to painfully strain at the oars (Mark 6:48). They soon realized they were in trouble, though not necessarily in danger of sinking. By the "fourth watch" (sometime early in the morning), these experienced oarsmen had covered only three or four miles (John 6:19). The lake itself was only seven miles across at its widest part.

But since they were out there in obedience to Christ's command, He would supply them with what they needed to carry out their mission. And then, amid the disciples' fears and struggles, Jesus went out to them, walking on the water. Such miraculous walking is another unique sign that Jesus is fully God. Isaiah 43:16 describes Him as the God who "makes a way in the sea, a path in the mighty waters." Job 38:16 says He is the God who "entered into the springs of the sea, or walked in the recesses of the deep."

Not at first recognizing the figure of Jesus (either due to the storm or because of dimness of the light that night), the disciples panicked, fearing the presence of a demon or ghost that was about to overtake the boat.

Immediately, Jesus identified Himself, shouting out words of encouragement: (Matthew 14:27) "Take heart; it is I. Do not be afraid."

Peter immediately responded to the friendly voice of Jesus, (Matthew 14:28–29) "Lord, if it is You, command me to come to You on the water." "Come," Jesus encouraged him.

Courageous and confident, Peter desired to imitate His Lord. While Peter focused on Christ, he was not engulfed in the raging waters (Matthew 14:29). Matthew did not tell us how long Peter was able to do this. We are only informed that fear over the circumstances around Peter overtook him, and at that moment he began to sink. But wisely, Peter cried out, "Lord, save me" (Matthew 14:30). Immediately, Jesus' hand upheld Peter and he was not submerged beneath the water (Matthew 14:31).

So often, Jesus' followers, like Peter, forget to retain their focus upon Jesus' invitation. When out of the Christ-focus, they soon find themselves caught in the struggle of faith with fear! To Peter and all the other followers of Christ, Jesus said, (Matthew 14:31) "O you of little faith, why did you doubt?"

As Jesus and Peter got into the boat, the wind ceased, and immediately the boat was at its destination (John 6:21). Psalm 107:28–31 describes distracted sailors who are brought to their "desired haven" by "the wondrous works" of the Lord.

Afterward, the disciples in the boat expressed their astonishment at what had just happened. They honored Christ, saying, (Matthew 14:33) "Truly You are the Son of God." That was their way of acknowledging Him as the Messiah. Even with this confession, they were still utterly astounded at what Jesus was able to do.

But these disciples were in much need of the power of God's Spirit, since Mark's account informs us that "their hearts were hardened" (Mark 6:52). More than awe-inspiring miracles are required for a person to be convinced of the true nature of Jesus' messiahship and to be able to walk unafraid through life's stormy waters.

Christian tradition has perceived this story of the disciples' boat being tossed by the waves and the wind as an image of the struggling church "between two shores," fighting the tide of evil. The Church on earth is the suffering Church, under the sign of the cross and in the dark of night in Jesus' seeming absence. Yet, believers are challenged to exhibit faith because they hear Jesus' words still calling to His people, (Mark 6:50) "Take heart; it is I. Do not be afraid."

## 5 Materials Made Vehicles with Sacramental Blessings

As in the exodus desert wandering, when God assured His people of His continuing guidance by a special cloud by day and a pillar of fire by night, so today God gives His people visuals that sign, seal, and deliver His guiding presence.

As God incarnate, Jesus continued this confirmation when He created special rituals that united God's words of promise with visual actions. These sacraments take into account that we are human, a unity of the physical and the spiritual. They are God's visible signs to the human senses: to our hearing, seeing, smelling, tasting, and touching. Certain earthly elements deliver unique heavenly blessings to all who receive them. They give Christians their citizenship in the new creation and nourish them on their earthly journey to that new creation.

Talking to the prominent Pharisee Nicodemus, Jesus gave this heavenly statement, (John 3:5) "Truly, truly I say to you, unless one is born of water and the Spirit, he cannot enter the kingdom of God." Jesus is talking about Baptism. We know this from the context, because prior to this conversation, the Pharisees sent an investigation team to inquire why John the Baptizer was baptizing (John 1:24–25). Moreover, after Jesus' private conversation with Nicodemus, Jesus went to the countryside to baptize (John 3:22). Then, to the Samaritan woman, who offered Jesus her "empty bucket," Jesus promised to fill it with His special "living water" (John 4:10). The living water is the Holy Spirit (John 7:38–39).

Baptismal water is like an envelope that delivers the Holy Spirit to the one being baptized. Because the Spirit is not sexist, nor guilty of age discrimination, He brings anyone of either sex, and from infant to aged, into a new status before God. He delivers the baptized from the kingdom of Satan and gives them a spiritual rebirth into a family created by Jesus' death and resurrection.

God also uses bread and wine (which rabbis would call the "blood of the grape") as vehicles that bring Jesus' historical body and blood, the same body that was once crucified but now glorified, into union with all participants in a sacred fellowship meal. The unity of God's Word and earthly elements create a "Holy Communion" between Jesus Christ and the communicants, as well as a bond of spiritual fellowship of the communicants with one another.

Jesus identifies the unleavened bread and the cup of wine with His body and blood (Matthew 26:26–28). Because the relationship of the bread and wine to Jesus' historical body is unique to this sacramental meal, it is called Jesus' "sacramental presence." In this sacred meal, Jesus is present bodily in a way that is mysteriously different from Jesus' general presence as Lord of creation.

Likewise, Jesus told His disciples—and us!—to partake of the cup of wine, "the blood of the grape," that He distributes for this joyous celebration (Matthew 26:28a).

Jesus linked this special meal with His coming self-sacrifice on the cross when He said, (Matthew 26:28) "This is My blood of the [new] covenant, which is poured out for many for the forgiveness of sins" (see Matthew 27:25; John 19:34). According to Exodus 24:8, the blood poured out at the base of the temple's altar was also sprinkled upon the assembled worshipers to seal the covenant fellowship between God and the people. In a greater way, Jesus' sacrificial blood now brings communion and reconciliation between God and sinners (1 Corinthians 10:16).

### Conclusion

In Jesus Christ, God's Son on earth, we witness the exercise of the power of the Creator, not like that of a bully to intimidate those who are weaker, but like that of a caring father who desires to bring his dependent children joy, confidence, and inner calmness. He understands and aids them, sometimes in a way that they feel His hand directly (miracle), but often in the quiet daily feeding from Word and Sacrament amid the dangers, bruises, and fears His children face as they grow toward spiritual maturity and their eternal home.

## Concluding Activities

Pray aloud: Blessed are You, O Lord, King of the universe. Blessed are You! We, Your dependent children, offer to You our awe and appreciation for the many strengthening delivery systems with which You surround us. In Word and Sacrament, You sustain us amid our pilgrim struggles and fears that we may arrive safely home with You in eternity, O Father, Son, and Holy Spirit. Amen.

Make any necessary announcements and distribute study leaflet 8.

# Caring for Creation

## Genesis 1:26, 28; 2:15; Philippians 3:12–14; 4:5; 1 Peter 2:12–3:7; Luke 16:1–13

*Preparing for the Session*

## Central Focus

Aware of their being given the privilege of being over creation as its trustee, Christians work hard to preserve the fruitfulness of the earth and all that is necessary for the continued existence of humanity on earth. This trusteeship includes Christians developing the energy of the mind with all its strength and becoming the disciplined spiritual athletes God intends them to be. The Christians' mission is to represent the caring Christ in all areas of life, home, workplace, and government. Appreciative of the world's goods rightly obtained, Christians will use them to support creative methods for world evangelism.

## Objectives

That participants, led by the Holy Spirit working through God's Word, will

1. take responsibility for governing the earth's resources in a caring manner on God's behalf;

2. take control of their body and mind so as to reflect what God's redemption of them implies; and

3. adopt a lifestyle that influences culture for the better in all its aspects.

**Note for the small-group leaders:** Lesson notes and other materials you will need begin on page 74.

## For the Lecture Leader

*Session Plan*

### Worship

Begin the session with the hymn printed in the study leaflet. Accompaniments are available in denominational hymnals, such as *Lutheran Service Book* or *Lutheran Worship* (refer to hymnal index). (Note: Concordia Publishing House has available *The Concordia Organist*. All the initial worship hymns in the LifeLight courses are included in this resource. It's especially helpful for mission congregations and small parishes. See the list of study resources on page 7.) Follow with this prayer:

### Prayer

O most Holy Trinity, Creator, Redeemer, and the unity behind all creation, give us eyes to see the privilege and responsibility that we have to walk on the earth as Your caring representatives. Help us to use the limited resources of the planet in such a way that they will benefit humans, who are the greatest resource You have created. Through whatever work You enable us to do, and with whatever material wealth we obtain, keep our values in the proper order, with You always first in what we fear, love, and trust. We ask this in the name of Jesus Christ, true God and true man, creation's Lord and our Redeemer. Amen.

## Lecture Presentation

### Introduction

People today are aware of the degradations of the planet's land and water, deforestation, and species extinction. Because of this degradation, many people want a lifestyle change that makes them "green" consumers, meaning they want to use products that are environmentally friendly.

Christians appreciate and support actions that seek to replenish the earth's limited resources and call human persons to responsible trusteeship of creation. Psalms 24:1 and 50 testify that all the earth is still the Lord's, including its animals and plants. Jesus spoke of the sun as "His" [God's] sun (Matthew 5:45). Moreover, it is God who feeds the birds and clothes the lilies and gives the grass of the field (Matthew 6:26, 28, 30).

Sadly, human sin causes a "bulldozer" mentality that ravages the land of its limited resources and causes creation to groan (Romans 8:22). But the Son of God's visit to the planet brought human redemption, and He will bring about creation's eventual restoration (as the next session will underline). Aware of this good news, Christians, like the moon that reflects the sun in our galaxy, seek to be reflectors of Christ, the Son of God, in how they use all resources of the earth in a caring way.

## 1 Responsible Caretakers (Genesis 1:26, 28; 2:15)

1:26, 28—While "nature" is not divine, it is God's handiwork. Human beings are connected to the rest of the physical universe through their physical nature. To human beings, God gave the ability to respond to the gift of creation, thereby making them accountable before God for how they use that gift. God gave us the privilege and responsibility of exercising "lordship" over the material or nonhuman world. Because God has given humans the honor of subduing the earth, modern science can be viewed as a tool God provided to humanity for the access and control of creation's treasures. Concerning his own work, Galileo, one of the first modern scientists, said that he was, "thinking God's thoughts after Him."

Because sin permeates all human existence, people sometimes turn technology into a tyrant that enslaves and destroys as much as it serves humanity. Human beings, therefore, in prayer and thanksgiving, seek to learn from God's Word how they are to make good use of the earth's resources (1 Timothy 4:4).

2:15—Human "lordship," being rulers, having "dominion," is not the same as a dictatorship. "Lordship" over creation entails caring for it and particularly for humankind, as God does. God's placement of Adam into Eden as its gardener serves to remind Adam's descendants of their duties to represent God as they protect what He created. Psalm 8:6 reaffirms God's mandate to those created and their delegated responsibility for creation: "You have given him dominion over the works of Your hands." This task of responsible stewardship in exercising dominion gives purpose and meaning to a person's existence on planet earth.

Jesus described the nature of human lordship when He told His followers that they were to serve others (Mark 10:43–44). God's people can serve Him by helping their neighbors. This helping our neighbors includes the kind of constructive participation that preserves human life and protects the natural environment, because every human is dependent upon the earth's limited resources for physical and economic health. We are to avoid and oppose anything that undermines the capacity of the earth to keep on thriving.

## 2 Confident Caretakers (Philippians 3:12–14)

When God's people care for creation, they do so out of love for God and their neighbor (Mark 12:29–31). Christians must adopt the attributes of a winning athlete, as Paul reminds the Philippians. God has placed Christians in a marathon race. In order to participate in the ancient Greek marathon, the athlete had to be a citizen. However, he did not run the race to gain citizenship. Nor do Christians run the race God puts them in in order to be saved. Christ has already established their citizenship in the coming new creation (Philippians 3:20).

Aware of the privilege they have of representing God's team, Christians have the responsibility, and the Holy Spirit's power, to "press on" faithfully wherever God has positioned them. Each believer, with his or her own special gifts from God, has a special lane on the track in which to run, and each has a goal to achieve. Until the time when that race is over, there are essential things God's athletes need to have to stay on track.

Verse 12—First is a God-given dissatisfaction. As works in progress, Christians are not satisfied with their level of service to the Lord. Paul affirmed this when he commented, "not that I have already attained this." Christians are not satisfied with the extent to which they are using the Word in their lives to reflect Christ's glory. Thus, they press on and continue to build upon the victories and obstacles that lead toward the goal.

Verse 13—Second is devotion to the Lord's work. Paul stressed this in the words "But one thing I do." At times, Christians may devote too much energy to nonessential things. They need to remember that no athlete succeeds by doing everything. He succeeds by specializing. It is a matter of values and priorities. It is living for God, who matters most.

Third is direction. Paul writes that he is "forgetting what lies behind." We cannot erase the mistakes of the past, but we can change the meaning of the past by seeing it in the light of Christ's accomplishments, which move us forward to a blessed future. Paul wrote, (Romans 8:1) "There is therefore now no condemnation for those who are in Christ Jesus."

Verse 14—Fourth is determination. Paul writes, "I press on toward the goal for the prize of the upward call of God in Christ Jesus." The Greek word for "press on" was used to describe a hunter eagerly pursuing his prey. There is a purpose and wonderful destiny with a name on it for every Christian, and he or she hangs on to it by faith with all his or her strength. At the end, the winner in the Greek games was summoned from the floor of the arena up to the judge's seat for the prize. Possibly, Paul was referring to this custom. "The upward call," was the signal Paul was awaiting that would bring him into the presence of Christ to receive the recognition of his triumph (2 Timothy 4:7–8).

Fifth is discipline. The runner must also obey the rules. In the Greek games, the judges were very strict about this. Any infringement of the rules disqualified the athlete. He did not lose his citizenship, but he did lose his privilege to participate and win the prize. Hebrews 12:1 has this exhortation: "Let us also lay aside every weight, and sin which clings so closely, and let us run with endurance the race that is set before us."

## 3 Dominion of the Mind (Philippians 4:5)

Proverbs 23:6–7 highlights the importance of our interior life. In other words, a person becomes what he or she thinks. In Matthew 22:37, Jesus said the mind, as well as the heart and soul is under the lordship of our God. For this reason, the apostle Paul, in his Letter to the Philippians, uses the words *mind* ten times and *think* five times, as well as forms of the word *remember* several times.

Paul encourages Christians to (Philippians 4:5) "Rejoice in the Lord always; again I will say, Rejoice." Twice Paul gives this exhortation because he knows there are times when personal resources and sorrows around us offer very little reasons for rejoicing. (Paul himself was in prison when he wrote this.) Nevertheless, a Christian's joy is real because it is "in the Lord," who, as Romans 8:28 says, works everything for the good of His people. As an encouragement to rejoice in the Lord, Paul reminds readers that the Lord is near and always present to aid (Philippians 4:5).

But accompanying that external reality of the Lord's presence is something internal, a mind-set in us. The Christian mind-set is both realistic and yet not pessimistic. The mental attitude Scripture calls each Christian to develop in order to exhibit the joy that is the fruit of the Holy Spirit is not only accepting one's limitations as a sinner (1 John 1:8) but also exercising one's strength as a forgiven sinner, a member of God's family through Baptism.

Certainly, one's status from the Christ-connection does not eliminate suffering from the believer's life. Jesus Christ knew plenty of grief and suffering. Nevertheless, when Jesus saw the coming horrors of the cross, He was still able to say to His followers, (John 15:11) "These things I have spoken to you, that My joy may be in you, and that *your* [emphasis added] joy may be full."

For the inner joy of Christians to be strengthened, Paul encourages believers to be people of prayer; taking "everything" that concerns them into God's presence, confident that He will take care of them. With that attitude, they can already offer up "thanksgiving" for His relief (Philippians 4:6). Thereby, their prayer becomes an act of worship.

Christians are realistic that without Christ they are simply sinners. But they are no longer pessimistic sinners, because with Christ they are forgiven and gifted with His righteousness. Christians *are* spiritually alive in Christ to be His lights and His letters to the world that needs a new message for a certain hope. A mind-set on the Christian's value in Christ enables them even now to a life of confident joy.

## 4 Contributing to Creation (1 Peter 2:12–3:7)

2:12—Jesus is holy, and yet He involved Himself in the day-to-day cares of a sinful world (Luke 15:1–2)—not only while at worship in the temple and synagogue but also in the marketplace, on public roads, and at weddings and banquets. The apostle Peter helps us to be also in the world, useful to our society, without becoming pagan ("Gentiles") in lifestyle (1 Peter 2:12a).

But because Christians are truly different in the way they act on the job, in social situations, or even at home, outsiders will perceive them as troublemakers, "evildoers"(v. 12b). Church history informs us that many citizens of the Roman Empire were socially hostile to Christians, viewing them as "people haters" because they would not participate in any athletic games that opened with prayers to pagan gods; nor would Christians attend live stage performances, which often were immoral.

2:13–15—But the best defense against a culture's suspicion and even hostility is a blameless life. A Christian's lifestyle is often used by God to lead to the conversion of onlookers.

Christians are not anarchists; Christians are law-abiding citizens. If the law of one's government violates the revealed will of God, one can look to the example of the Early Christians who, when some Roman emperors wanted them to prove their loyalty to the empire by worshiping the emperor, refused to do so and suffered martyrdom as a result. Underlying Christians' submission to being good citizens is their commitment to Christ; they obey "for the Lord's sake." Knowing what the proper hierarchy within creation is, Christians recognize that God is to be feared, while the emperor is simply to be honored (v. 17).

2:16–17—As living servants of God, Christians add value to any society in which they live. In four brief social commands, Peter exhorts Christians to "honor everyone." Christians are to recognize the worth of every human life and give to each human being—regardless of age, race, or economic condition—due respect as God's creature. Moreover, Christians are to engage in deliberate acts of love towards other Christians, "the brotherhood" of believers.

2:18—Christians are to be good employees. Peter addresses Christians who are also household slaves. Their submission and obedience to their masters is to be done "with all respect." Rather than complaining, they are to be cooperative, because they are to be conscious of God's presence and will in their lives (see Luke 6:35–36). Christ's self-sacrificing ministry underlines Christian slaves' submission to their employers (vv. 22–25). Serving faithfully under bad "bosses," the Christian slave will be their "Suffering Servant" Lord.

2:23–24—Christ, too, though innocent, suffered. Paradoxically, through the hurt done to Christ came the healing of the spiritual wounds of those who are His spiritual sheep.

3:1–2—Peter begins the next chapter with advice to wives, especially those who have pagan husbands. Peter's statement "without a word" refers to the influence of a wife's godly lifestyle. What her lips cannot accomplish through direct evangelism, her lifestyle, being "chaste and respectful," will.

3:3–4—Paul warns against the fashions of the pagans, saying that Christian wives are to avoid extravagant ornamentation. Christian women are to be living witnesses of an inner beauty of the heart and a gentle disposition that reflects Jesus, who also praised this character (see Matthew 11:29; 5:5).

3:5–6—Like ancient Sarah, who showed a wife's proper deference to her husband, Abraham, so a Christian wife is to be obedient to her husband, continuing in well doing and quietness. By their obedience, Christian wives will help remove from among their pagan neighbors any suspicion that Christians undercut the social fabric.

3:7—Peter "likewise" addresses Christian husbands. They are to live with their wives "in an understanding way"; that is, with the Christian vision that is formed by their knowledge that they are equal recipients of God's grace, as are their wives. The husband must be sensitive to his wife's needs so that they can pray together in a way that pleases God. See Matthew 5:23–24 and Isaiah 1:10–17, which talk about the importance of being agents of reconciliation. This is especially important in the family.

## 5 Managing One's Material Resources (Luke 16:1–13)

As it is a mistake to equate poverty with piety, so also it is a mistake to equate riches with lack of righteousness. A person of faith is expected to also be an astute person financially. Some pastors hesitate to mention the money that Christians should be giving to the church's mission in the world. Nice ideas get nowhere if bills are not paid and Christian churches and schools then must close their doors.

But God's biblical leaders had no such hesitancy in asking believers to give generously of their earthly goods. Moses asked people to give gold and other gifts to build the tabernacle (Exodus 35:5). Jesus paid the yearly temple tax for the upkeep of the worship services in the temple (Matthew 17:27), and He commended a widow for her sacrificial offering in the temple (Luke 21:1–3). Paul devoted three chapters in his Corinthian epistles to the subject. During his missionary journeys, he collected money from Gentile believers to pay for food for starving Jerusalem Christians (Acts 11:27–30).

Verses 1–2—Jesus expects Christians to be wise money managers. He affirmed this in His story of a rich absentee landlord. The man had a manager for his estate who acted as his legal agent. Someone informed the landlord that his manager had neglected his responsibilities. The boss called in his manager to give an accounting of the value of the property entrusted to him, for he was about to be replaced.

Verses 3–4—Thinking quickly, the manager resolved to make plans for his future, since he was unable to see any further chance of employment here. Suddenly an idea came to him as to how his employer's creditors could take care of his future. Verses 5–7—Because secrecy was essential, the estate manager summoned his master's debtors one by one and rewrote their bills. What he most likely reduced on the bill was his commission, rather than what was owed the estate owner.

Verse 8a—When the estate owner heard about the way

the manager dealt with his personal crisis, the owner commended the manager, not for his previous wastefulness, and certainly not for any type of dishonesty, but rather for having acting shrewdly in the current crisis the manager had found himself.

Verses 8b–13—Jesus then tells the disciples how they are to apply the parable to themselves. But first, Jesus reprimands them for not being as alert as non-Christians in regard to how their material possessions are to be used. Often, non-Christians are more shrewd users of their material possessions for selfish gain than Christians tend to be, but for the right reasons. Jesus does not consider naiveté in business practices to be an acceptable ingredient in piety or in order for Christians to be nonworldly. Regarding Christians' business practices, Jesus said, (v. 9) "I tell you, make friends for yourselves by means of unrighteous wealth, so that when it fails [either at the time we die or when the world is brought to an end] they may receive you into the eternal dwellings."

Verses 10–13—Then Jesus drew a secondary application. His followers are to be faithful. If they are unwise with such little things as money, they are likely to be unwise in their most critical possession, eternal life. A Christian's giving to the Church's outreach with the Gospel to the world is a testimony to the reality of his or her discipleship and self-denial, as well as the desire to use things in the service of God above all else.

What a person is willing to give up—especially in the matter of earthly things—is often the true portrait of the inner self. Jesus says, (v. 13a) "No servant can serve two masters." Those who worship mammon—material wealth—serve it totally. Those who worship God, likewise, must serve Him totally. Tragically, those who serve worldly things often do so more energetically and more shrewdly than those who are followers of Christ.

While remaining alert to the power of possessions to possess those who devote themselves to them, nevertheless, Christians want to do the best in whatever they do, and sometimes doing so leads to material wealth. What God still looks at is the attitude one has for becoming wealthy. It is to be that of gratitude for God's own commitment to us, to His grace that freed us from the greatest poverty, the debt to sin (2 Corinthians 5:14; 8:9). In gratitude to such a Creator comes the Christian's mission statement to be in a "partnership" with God in His ongoing work of building the kingdom of God (Philippians 1:5).

We each have only one life, and only what we do in that life for Christ will last (Revelation 14:13). A life lived in faithful partnership with God will receive praise from God, who manages the largest corporation in existence, the universe. To those who understand that their net worth is not a valid standard of their self-worth, money is considered like foreign currency. Christians value more their citizenship in the new creation, and that makes their existence of eternal worth (Philippians 3:20; 2 Timothy 4:6, 8).

### Conclusion

God leaves His redeemed people in the world to benefit all its creatures, be they mighty or weak, human or even nonhuman. Acknowledging that we are in a relationship not only with God but also with the earthly environment, we Christians will be good stewards of the earth's physical assets. Among these assets are Christians themselves. Like disciplined athletes, Christians will guard their inner life from the morally questionable and remain focused on their baptismal status and the victory that being "in Christ" gives to them.

## Concluding Activities

Pray aloud: Dear heavenly Father, in gratitude for our redemption through Your Son, and confident that You have sent us Your Holy Spirit in Word and Sacrament, we ask that You enable us this day to be faithful trustees of Your various gifts in creation. You have saved us by Your grace; use us, we pray, as instruments of Your grace. Show us how to be wise in the use of our wealth and work so as to be true partners in Your providential care of life on earth. Most of all, lay upon our hearts and energize our spirits to use our time, talents, and treasures in support of bringing Christ to the nations for their salvation. Amen.

Make any necessary announcements and distribute study leaflet 9.

# The New Creation

## 2 Peter 3; Matthew 24:29; 25:31–46; Revelation 21:1–22:5; 1 Thessalonians 4

*Preparing for the Session*

### Central Focus

The present state of the universe, with the presence of sin and its negative impact, will end one day. Christians patiently wait for Christ to usher in the new universe, which will be without sin but will have, for all those who trust in Christ, the never-ending secure blessing of unobstructed fellowship with the triune God and with all God's faithful, resurrected people.

### Objectives

That participants, led by the Holy Spirit working through God's Word, will

1. be patient with God for still allowing sin and suffering in the world, even among His faithful people;
2. be confident that a future of unending joy and fellowship with God and all the faithful departed awaits them; and
3. be enabled for a lifestyle that reflects that of people who know that their future is with the triune God.

**Note for the small-group leaders:** Lesson notes and other materials you will need begin on page 77.

### For the Lecture Leader

*Session Plan*

#### Worship

Begin the session with the hymn printed in the study leaflet. Accompaniments are available in denominational hymnals, such as *Lutheran Service Book* or *Lutheran Worship* (refer to hymnal index). (Note: Concordia Publishing House has available *The Concordia Organist*. All the initial worship hymns in the LifeLight courses are included in this resource. It's especially helpful for mission congregations and small parishes. See the list of study resources on page 7.) Follow with this prayer:

#### Prayer

Dear heavenly Father, open our eyes to see beyond the sin and suffering of our present life to that unobstructed joy and fellowship we will have with You and all our faithful departed loved ones, who are kept safely in the hands of our Lord and Savior, Jesus Christ. Enable us by Your Holy Spirit so that even now we will reflect the life of holiness of the coming new creation as we await the resurrection of the dead and the life of the world to come. Confident that in Christ the way to the fullness of eternal life is ours, we pray this day. Amen.

### Lecture Presentation

#### Introduction

Waiting can be a very difficult thing. We have probably all experienced that. It can be hard to wait for something we really want. We have all heard that a watched pot never boils, and sometimes that really seems like the truth. It seems that the more we want something, the longer we have to wait for it.

While that is true of mundane, earthly things, it is especially true of eternal, heavenly things. Our fallen state and the continued presence of evil in the world around us cause us to long for the life of the world to come. We read in Romans 8 that this longing and waiting is true not just of ourselves but also of all of creation: (v. 23) "For we know that the whole creation has been groaning together in the pains of childbirth until now." The whole created world waits with us for the final restoration and re-creation that will occur when our Lord Christ returns on the Last Day.

## 1 Scoffers of the Coming End (2 Peter 3)

Verses 1–2—While we wait, we are called on to trust in the promises of God in Christ and to strive to live as He would have us. The seriousness of living the godly lifestyle and watching out for the corrupters of the apostolic message is based upon the certainty of a day of eternal judgment. Peter's second epistle seeks to remind us of the prediction about the coming of scoffers who doubt God's Word.

Verses 3–10—Peter explains that there are some who are turning the delay in Christ's return into an occasion for ridiculing it. But these scoffers ignore the fact that creation is the work only of God, and He alone determines when He will destroy it. God once before destroyed this world by the great flood (v. 6). God will destroy the earth again "for fire" on the Last Day (v. 7).

Those who deny that God will end the present creation do not have the proper perspective of history. They do not know the God of eternity, who brought earth time into existence. His endless time is not that of human time. Even Second Peter's recipients, in order not to lose patience, need to be reminded (v. 8) "that with the Lord one day is as a thousand years, and a thousand years as one day" from eternity's perspective (see also Psalm 90:4).

Christ's delay of His visible return to judge all people is actually an act of His mercy and not evidence of an indifference to His promised coming. The delay exhibits His love, patience, and desire to have all people repent and receive His salvation. In any case, Christ's coming to judge all will surely come, even though its timing is both unknown and unexpected by the nonrepentant.

Verses 11–18—In view of the approaching judgment, and the new creation that Christ will usher in at that time, what sort of people ought Christians be? Peter answers, (v. 14) "Therefore, beloved, since you are waiting for these, be diligent to be found by Him without spot or blemish, and at peace." The Christians' present life is meant to reflect their citizenship in the coming new creation, wherein only righteousness will dwell. As 1 John 3:2–3 also states, "Beloved, we are God's children now, and what we will be has not yet appeared; but we know that when He appears we shall be like Him, because we shall see Him as He is. And everyone who thus hopes in Him purifies himself as He is pure." As we await the new creation, we are not to lose patience, but we are to take as our example the patient hope of our Lord, as well as the example set by "our beloved brother Paul" (2 Peter 3:15).

Christians are to be anticipating, doctrinally aware, and doctrinally correct people who resist spiritual errors of every type, especially those connected with the present universe's end. Certainly, Scripture study on the end times is difficult. Even if such matters are hard to understand, Christians must take them seriously, as they do "the other Scriptures" (v. 16).

To grow in the knowledge of God's grace and wisdom keeps one not only upon the safe, lighted path to eternal salvation but also leads one to praise the person who is that path, (v. 18) "our Lord and Savior Jesus Christ. To Him be the glory both now and to the day of eternity. Amen."

## 2 The Great Separation at the Final Judgment (Matthew 24:29; 25:31–46)

24:29—When Jesus comes to end the present state of the universe, that event will be unmistakable, as all the people of the earth will see the physical elements of the universe changing.

25:31–32—To the joy of Christians—but to the dismay of doubters—Jesus' divine majesty will be fully seen as His angels escort Him as the undisputed king of heaven and earth to His throne of judgment. Everyone will then be brought before God's judgment throne, now in their resurrection bodies.

25:33—Speaking metaphorically to His followers, Jesus described a mixed flock of sheep and goats. To understand Jesus' metaphor, we need to know that in the evening Jewish shepherds would separate the goats from the sheep because the goats had to be kept warm. Speaking metaphorically, Jesus said, "And He [God] will place the sheep on His right, but the goats on the left." The ancient world considered one's right side to be the place of both power and honor.

25:34—During His earthly ministry, Jesus' enemies called Him "king" only in derision. But at the great separation of humanity on the Last Day, all people will acknowledge His lordship. Jesus, however, will call Himself "King" only to those on His "right." Only to them will Jesus extend the invitation to inherit "the kingdom prepared for [them] from the foundation of the world." Even before the universe was created, God the Father had planned to bring sinners into a blessed relationship with Him through the ministry of His Son (see Ephesians 1:4).

25:35–36—Jesus, the King and Judge, explains the reason for the blessing to those at His right.

25:37–39—Since this is the *public* judgment, Jesus directs attention to the visible works that His "sheep" had done while living in the old creation. These works are decisive in the final judgment because of their evidential quality, not because of any inherent merit. Jesus explicitly described those who are saved as "the righteous." They have trusted in Jesus' own righteousness rather than their own. As they extended hospitality to others, cared for the hungry, thirsty, foreigners, naked, sick, and imprisoned, the believers were actually serving the ministry of Jesus because of their gratitude for what He had done for them.

25:40—Only the "blessed" and "righteous" are citizens of King Jesus' kingdom. To them He says, "Truly, I say to you, as [to the extent that] you did it to one of the least of these My brothers, you did it to Me." The good deeds of the righteous follow them into eternity, where God graciously rewards (Revelation 14:13).

25:41—On the other hand, those "goats" on the "left" start with the delusion of having done big things that attracted the world's praise. But such self-centered people and their deeds receive God's rejection because they are not in a proper relationship to Him. Thus Jesus, their final judge, tells them, "Depart from Me, you cursed, into the eternal fire prepared for the devil and his angels."

But Jesus does not add the words "of my Father" after "cursed" when describing those on the left. They have brought the curse of eternal damnation upon themselves.

25:42–45—Previously, Jesus mentioned only the good deeds the saved did (vv. 35–40). Now Jesus mentions only those things that the damned did not do. They had failed to live in a way that recognized the gracious God behind all of their life. Again note Jesus' reference to Himself: "For I was hungry"; "I was thirsty"; etc. Such little deeds that the damned did not do are concrete evidence that they are spiritually disconnected from Jesus. While the righteous asked a "when" question three times, caused by the humbleness of their faith, now the condemned also ask "when" (v. 44). They do so only once and in a spirit of reprimand and reproach. They want to blame the Lord (finally acknowledging that He is "Lord" but it is too late).

## 3 Visions of the New Creation (Revelation 21:1–22:5)

21:1–4—God has not ceased being sole ruler over creation. Satan and sin's presence in creation will not stop God's good plans for creation from being consummated. Christians are optimistic people because Scripture has told them that the best blessings from God are yet to come to them. For the glorious spiritual bodies of the resurrected saints, God will also give a new universe.

According to Revelation 21:1, John saw a "new" (Greek: *kainos*) heaven and earth (echoing the poetic words of Isaiah 65:17; 66:22). The Greek word *kainos* designates something that already existed but now appears in a new aspect.

While the hell of unbelievers will be the experience of being utterly alone, that will not be the everlasting state of Christ's people, for that state will have wonderful social dimensions. This is affirmed Revelation 21:1b: "the sea was no more." For God's ancient people, the sea symbolized a place of separation and isolation, as well as the turbulent spiritual realm out of which the terrible persecuting beast rose. Moreover, the sea was the thing that shut John off and separated him from his beloved fellow Christians. In the new creation, all believers will have the fellowship of the angels (Hebrews 12:22) and conscious fellowship and reunion with departed believers (Matthew 8:11; Luke 13:29). Best of all, Satan, who has already been conquered through Christ's cross, will no longer trouble Christ's people, who have unchallenged fellowship with God (John 14:3; Colossians 1:19–21). There is no more death: "the former things have passed away" (Revelation 21:4–5). The new creation is without the ravages of sin, death, or evil.

21:5—For the first and only time in the Book of Revelation, God the Father Himself speaks. He does so as absolute Lord over all, to ratify what has just been written. Despite the suffering all around His people, God is even now creating a new world. Mysteriously, under divine wisdom, there is a connection between the present suffering of God's people and the future world God is shaping.

21:6—For the "thirsty" (believers who desire God; Isaiah 55:1), God will freely quench that thirst by the grace of Christ and the gift of the Holy Spirit within them.

21:10–11—The eternal blessing of the eternal state of the redeemed Church is seen as "the holy city Jerusalem coming down out of heaven from God." The city shines with the radiance of God's presence.

21:12–14—The new creation will never again be under attack from evil. Verse 12 mentions a great "high wall." In the ancient world, a high wall symbolized security and strength for a city. In this New Jerusalem, there is easy entrance provided by the twelve gates, three on each side. Twelve angels stand at the gates, but not to bar the way as in Eden. Now angels show the redeemed the way into the city, from whatever direction they are coming. This is the universal, worldwide Church. According to verse 14, the wall had twelve foundations (see Ephesians 2:20). The new world is built upon the witness of the apostles, who carried on when ethnic Israel had failed.

21:18–21—The wall around the eternal city, its gates, and its foundations are made of jewels. The jewels symbolize that the New Jerusalem is a place of purity and durability that will last forever.

22:1–2—The wonderful structure of the New Jerusalem and the blessedness of the new life of its inhabitants are portrayed in these verses. Life is abundant everywhere. Perfect life from God streams unceasingly through the renewed world. God's people finally are forever free of the negatives of their former existence with sin and its many consequences. The angel showed John the "river of the water of life," symbolic of eternal life that satisfies all human thirst-needs because its source is God, who made Christians to be the earthly reflection of His goodness and had redeemed them through "the Lamb." On each side of the river stands "the tree of life." It is watered by the crystal stream that flows from God's throne (a possible reference to the Holy Spirit's creative work). The healing leaves of the tree of life have overcome all sickness—sickness is no more. This does not mean that it will be possible for the people of the new creation to get sick, but that the water of life produces health and strength to all in its midst.

22:2–3—A chief source of blessing to the citizens of the New Jerusalem is that they are no longer under sin's curse. After Adam and Eve had sinned, they were forbidden to eat from the tree of life so that they could not have eternal life as long as they were controlled by sin (Genesis 322–24). Now, however, because God's people have been freed from the control and consequences of sin through the Lamb, the tree of life is there for them all.

22:4–5—The renewed and purified faithful people can now look directly upon God, "see His face, and His name will be on their foreheads," meaning they are securely His family members. The good news for us who still wrestle against sin within and around us is that the darkness of deception and evil is banished forever. It is expressed in the words that the evil "night will be no more," for the Son of God's radiance is to be enjoyed in its fullness forever.

## 4 Living in the Light of the New Creation (1 Thessalonians 4)

Verses 1–2—Trust in Jesus Christ will not only bring the blessing of eternal fellowship with Him and other Christians from all cultures but will also even now create a new lifestyle among Christians living in the present creation. Paul describes several such lifestyles to the young missionary congregation in the area of Thessalonica.

Verses 3–8—First among the aspects of the different lifestyle that sets Christians apart from non-Christians is how Christians make use of God's gift of sexuality. Even though pagan philosophers warned against being slaves to passion, and even though various laws punished adultery, the pagans in Thessalonica were still too permissive toward sexual misconduct. As in contemporary motion pictures, television "soaps," paperback romance novels, and Internet pornography, so in ancient society there was a disconnect between one's religious views and how one dealt with sex.

However, Paul tells the Thessalonians, and thereby us today, to live a sexually pure life. The apostle placed special emphasis on the importance of maintaining moral purity in all associations between the sexes. Paul's words (v. 6) "no one transgress and wrong his brother in this matter" refer to marital infidelity, breaking into a brother's marriage by committing adultery with his wife. Though Paul is the great preacher of unconditional salvation through faith in Jesus Christ, nevertheless, he is also strong on declaring, "The Lord is an avenger in all these things." Such sins undermine a society's basic unit, the family. Good families are based on faithfulness between a husband and a wife and the sexual discipline that goes with it.

Verses 9–10—Second, while selfishness and a "me first" attitude create a divisive society, the Christian life is lived in appreciation of being a part of the society of forgiven sinners. Already, the young congregation at Thessalonica had a good reputation for exhibiting "brotherly love." Since they had been taught by God's Word how God poured out love abundantly through Christ upon sinners, Paul, as the Thessalonian Christians' spiritual father, can ask them to grow "more and more" in this love.

Verses 11–12—Such brotherly love is both comprehensive and practical. It is closely associated with personal holiness, with an inner calmness, and with the commitment to the proper performance of personal responsibilities. Consistent, daily work that makes an individual self-supporting and is conducive to the good order of society is an evidence of true love in a person. Those who so work do not place burdens on those around them. Thus "sloth," laziness that is unappreciative of life's opportunities, is sin. People of the Greco-Roman Empire looked down upon the individual who had to work for a living at some trade. In opposition to such a view, Paul insisted that the Christian should not be dependent upon the work of others.

Verses 13–15—Finally, the confidence Christians have that Jesus Christ has obtained victory over mortal man's last enemy, death, affects how they approach it. While some philosophers, such as Socrates, sought to prove that there was happiness after death, most of the pagan world had no word of assurance, no certain hope of a better life after death. This typical inscription on a pagan grave (perhaps influenced by Stoic philosophy) demonstrates this hopelessness: "I was not; I was. I am not; I don't care."

Verses 16–17—Certainly, death is a time of separation and a time of sorrow; nevertheless, whoever is placed in the hands of the living God is secure. Believers can be certain that God will change their good-byes to loved ones into hellos after the resurrection (see v. 17)!

With such confidence, the sorrow of a Christian over the death of a loved one does not lead to despair (v. 13). All believers (including those whom have already died) will be united together, walking in a triumphant parade with Christ at its head.

Whenever it is that God has determined to send Christ as judge, there is one thing of which Christians can be certain: they can look forward with rejoicing at His coming, for they will receive the full revelation of all His blessings for them, because they are people of that day (1 Thessalonians 5:5). A famous football "fight song" has the line "hail to the victors." Every human being is a player in a far more important "game," that of life itself. Not to get across the right goal of life means a defeat that is eternally damnable.

Christian evangelism is a call to all repentant sinners to join in the victory parade Christ heads. We can be certain of that victory, for we know that "in all these things we are more than conquerors though Him who loved us" (Romans 8:37). Those who trust in Christ are never victims, losers, or misfits. As King of kings and Lord of lords (Revelation 17:17), Jesus makes them members of His royal family (Revelation 1:6). "Hail to the victors!" is not limited to a university's football fight song; this is also a cheer that heaven's angels will shout joyfully, and even eternally, to Christians because Christ has made them the citizens of His new creation.

## Conclusion

Christians are realistic but not pessimistic people. They are aware of the daily need to guard against spiritual enemies in the present world, as well as the need to struggle with the "old Adam," the sinful nature still waging war within each believer against the Holy Spirit's work. Nevertheless, Christians, nourished by the Gospel's message of victory in Christ, are patient and hopeful people, confident that such warfare will one day end. Because they trust in Christ as the way, the truth, and the life, they see their life not as a dead-end street but as a pilgrimage toward the New Jerusalem, the city of joyous, unending fellowship with God and His people in the coming new creation.

## Concluding Activities

Pray aloud: Dear Heavenly Father, we thank You for all those You have saved by bring them to trust in Jesus Christ as their Savior and Lord. Thank You for giving to them and to us the enlightening power of the Holy Spirit so we may see Jesus Christ as not only the world's creator but also its only redeemer and final judge. We confidently wait for the time of Your ushering in the new creation, where we will have the unobstructed vision of Your immeasurable love for each of us. Living in the light of the life of eternity, we come to You this day as Your thankful people, and we joyfully await the summons to Your harvest home. Washed in the blood of Your Lamb, our Lord Jesus Christ, we commit our lives to even now exhibiting heaven's holiness. To Your most holy name we offer our praise forever more. Amen.

Make any necessary announcements (including, if possible, information about the next LifeLight course).

# Small-Group Leaders Material

Illustration by Sally Wern Comport

# The God of Creation

## Psalm 104:24–30; Genesis 1:1–25; Psalm 113:4–6; Genesis 11:1–9; Psalm 115:2–8

*Preparing for the Session*

## Central Focus

The universe and all that is in it is the result of the creative act of the triune God. The universe is not of the same essence of God, nor is anything in the universe to be given the fear, love, and trust that belongs only to God. The power, wisdom, goodness, and generosity of God seen in creation is meant to lead us to seek out the Creator so that we enter into a right relationship with the one God, who is the source of all existence.

## Objectives

That participants, led by the Holy Spirit working through God's Word, will

1. recognize that creation comes from the hand of a wise and generous Creator;

2. be alert to the temptation of fearing, loving, and trusting in things more than in God, their giver; and

3. share the good news that the greatest gift to creation is the triune God's redemption of it through the Son of God, who brings freedom from slavery to man-made idols, which cannot fulfill human need.

## For the Small-Group Leader

*Small-Group Discussion Helps*

### *Day 1* • Psalm 104:24–30

1. A non-Christian might see the Grand Canyon as simply the result of water erosion over millions of years, while the Christian might say how creative God has been in giving such beauty and wonders to behold.

2. In order to prove things scientifically, the scientific method must be followed. To prove the origin of the universe, several steps would have to be followed. First, a theory as to how the universe began would need to be formed. Second, experiments to demonstrate the truthfulness of the theory would have to be performed. Third, those experiments would have to be repeated to ensure that the results were accurate. Since no scientist has either the ability or the tools to duplicate again and again the creation of a universe, it is unlikely that science will ever be able definitively to demonstrate how the universe began. Some things are possible only for God.

3. We are all confronted with the existence of God our Creator in two basic ways. The first way is *externally*, by the power and grandeur of the world around us. The second way is *internally*, through the general concept of right and wrong, when we realize that there are certain things we ought to do and other things we are to avoid. Both of these things hint at the existence of a supreme Creator, a judge who holds every person responsible for his or her actions.

4. Such a great effect as the universe is, consisting of millions of stars and galaxies, must have a cause as great or greater. The universe's order and complexity testify to a great planner. As Hebrews 3:4 points out, a house does not just put itself together without a designer and builders.

5. While human beings are able to make things, they need tools or materials to produce those things. God, on the other hand, is able to create out of nothing. God simply speaks whatever He wants, and it comes into existence!

### *Day 2* • Genesis 1:1–25

6. The presence and activity of the Holy Spirit in the creation of the world is indicated to us in Genesis 1:2: "And the Spirit of God was hovering over the face of the waters."

7. The terms "sun" and "stars" may have been avoided in Genesis 1 because some ancient Middle East civilizations used such terms to describe their gods. Genesis stresses that the sun and stars are simply parts of creation that are useful but are not to be worshiped as gods.

8. God's work during the days of creation clearly shows us that He is the God of order. He created the land, then the plants upon it, and then the animals that depended upon those plants. All was done in order before the appearance of man.

9. The word in Genesis 1:11 that indicates that God gave vegetation and animals a mechanism for reproduction is "kind." The text states that God gave them all the ability to reproduce themselves; in other words, that each might produce more of itself (that is, more of its own kind).

10. Knowing that God intended all things to be good makes us appreciate that creation is to be enjoyed as a gift coming from the generous Creator, who asks us to seek His will in Scripture to learn how to use it for the good of all of God's creatures.

## *Day 3* • Psalm 113:4–6; Genesis 11:1–9

11. Our psalm clearly demonstrates that created things are not the same thing as God. Words in our text such as "high above" and "looks far down" show that God is differentiated, separate, and superior to any and all of the things that He made.

12. A creature is a thing that has existence only because the Creator, who is without beginning or ending, calls it into existence and sustains it.

13. Advances in technology can be beneficial things for which we should certainly give thanks to God. Each year, new things are invented and new products are made available to us that have the potential of improving our lives. However, we must remember that while technological advances can perform wonders in the natural world, they can never be an adequate substitute for the supernatural. In spite of the relative ease and convenience of modern life, we must always remember that the One who is infinitely superior to us provides for us and sustains us each day of our lives and even eternally.

14. First, we may see the material world as another good gift God gives us. Second, we are to thank Him for it. Third, we are to be in His presence through prayer and the study of His Word to see how we are to use His creation wisely.

15. The seemingly compulsive need to constantly purchase the newest, latest, and best is something that should concern us. May we always remember that acquiring material things can never satisfy the human spirit's need for communication with God. Ultimately, nothing else can ever satisfy or sustain us, for it is God alone who is the source of life in all its fullness. Through Christ Jesus, He freely gives us this life through His gifts of forgiveness and freedom from the ravages of sin.

## *Day 4* • Acts 14:8–17

16. Like the people at Lystra, we sometimes find it easy to expect too much of people we admire and forget that everyone has the fallibility and limitations of being only human and not God.

17. When the people of Lystra assumed that they were pagan gods, Paul and Barnabas tore their robes (probably at the seams, an ancient Jewish response to blasphemy), and then tried to prevent an animal from being sacrificed in their honor. In this way, they attempted to stop the people and point them to the Lord as the only true and living God.

18. We read in Scripture that the pagan gods are either nonexistent or actually demons instead ofgods.

19. God in His mercy regularly gives us many gifts to sustain us. He gives us all that we need to support this body and life. These gifts include sunshine, rain, and fertile ground. All of these things are necessary for food production and for our continued existence.

20. Our recognition of God's generosity and goodness in all that He provides for us through creation produces in us a gladness of heart and rejoicing in words of praise.

## *Day 5* • Psalm 115:2–8

21. Making a god is essentially a matter of trust. A "god" is something or someone that we trust to provide for us and ensure our ultimate security, joy, and deliverance from trouble.

22. Answers may vary. There is an endless list of things that people may turn to instead of God to provide for them. Certainly toward the top of that list, we would find money, education, and perhaps weapon systems. All of these are human attempts to find inner peace and security.

23. There are certain attributes of God that people do not like. These include His wrath and His jealousy. The jealousy of God should be understood as His zeal against all forms of idolatry that try to undermine His control over creation, because He alone has the power and wisdom for its survival.

24. When God considers the powerful of the earth, He sees them as being as fragile and vulnerable as grasshoppers that can easily be blown away.

25. We, who through our sinfulness are fallen creatures, freely receive reconciliation with God through our Re-

deemer, Jesus Christ. At Christ's Baptism, He identified with sinners in order to fulfill the righteousness that God requires of them. At His crucifixion, divine wrath and divine love met when the incarnate Son of God absorbed infinite wrath within His infinite mercy for fallen sinners (Romans 5:6).

# Creation of Man and Woman

## Genesis 1:26–2:25; Other Selected Passages

*Preparing for the Session*

### Central Focus

God's highest creation on the earth is man and woman. They are created for fellowship with God. As God's representatives over creation, they are to cultivate the earth's resources and, with the attitude of mutual respect, care and provide for those different from themselves. Moreover, man and woman, as husband and wife, are to be faithful and of mutual service to each other as they reflect the love of God, who in Jesus Christ is shown to be self-giving. Through constant dependence upon the God of creative love and constant fellowship with Him through Jesus Christ, each person's life reaches its fullest meaning.

### Objectives

That participants, led by the Holy Spirit working through God's Word, will

1. appreciate the value each person has as a unique creation of God;

2. work toward giving respect and support to all members of the human family; and

3. cherish the cultural diversity on earth but not accept the plurality of religions that do not confess Jesus Christ as the only path to a blessed eternity as equal with Christianity. .

### For the Small-Group Leader

*Small-Group Discussion Helps*

### *Day 1* • Genesis 1:26–27; Romans 5:17–20

1. It is important to understand that we are people specifically and intentionally created by God. If we thought that we were merely highly evolved animals, we would probably have much lower opinions of ourselves and of others around us. It would be easy to dismiss individuals' unique traits as the result of random chance and individuals themselves as largely irrelevant. Rather than leading lives of love and service, we might be tempted to lead lives more reflective of "survival of the fittest."

2. What is man? Do we truly have any value? These are important questions that affect our relationship with God and also how we regard one another. If people are simply objects, "its" rather than "you"s, then they can be manipulated for their votes or their money. The world becomes a savage place when any person—from an embryo in the womb to the aged person strapped in a wheelchair—is expendable without regret.

3. Christians must defend Adam and Eve as real because both Jesus and the apostle Paul turn to their existence to make theological assertions that affect all of us, such as the importance of marriage, our being sinners, and Jesus as the "second Adam" who saved us all.

### *Day 2* • Genesis 2:18–25

4. By looking at all the animals, Adam was led to see that he was qualitatively different from them and they were, therefore, not suitable companions to socialize with or to give great love to. The obvious conclusion was that he needed to rely on God to provide him with a suitable companion.

5. Adam's physical nature was formed out of the red clay of the earth, but Eve was taken from the already-formed nature of Adam.

6. A husband and wife are distinct persons. That is not obliterated when they become married. That distinction is celebrated, and the love between them respects those differences. The differences don't divide them because their self-giving love to each other unites them. In 2 Corinthians 13:14, we see that the Holy Spirit is the love that brings the Lover (God the Father) and the Beloved (God the Son) into the oneness of the Godhead. (These may be heavy thoughts, but they are eternally majestic and comforting.)

7. Headship of the husband is not a dictatorship that overrides the needs of the wife. Those who think dictatorial leadership is acceptable overlook Ephesians 5:29, which compares the husband's regard for his wife to Christ's self-sacrifice for His Bride, the Church.

8. Adam and Eve in Eden did not seek to obliterate their differences but saw them as comfortable signs of the reality that they were *inter*dependent (which is vastly

different from the often-selfish concept of being "independent").

## *Day 3* • Ephesians 5:22–33; Genesis 2:18–25

9. Marriage is not an institution that was dreamed up by society. It is not the result of any given cultural context. Rather, it is entirely God's creation and began with God taking the initiative in bringing Eve to Adam (Genesis 2:22).

10. In Ephesians 5:25, we see how highly God regards the estate of marriage. The relationship between husband and wife is compared with Christ's self-giving on Golgotha's cross, which washed sinners and made them His family and the Church His Bride.

11. In getting married, a man and woman leave their dependence upon their parents to commit themselves to the welfare of each other and the children that result from their physically becoming "one flesh."

12. The uniting of "flesh" that consummates the marriage is the uniting of two different sexes. By creating Eve, God created another gender clearly different from that of Adam. It is the joining together of people of these two different yet compatible genders that constituted a marriage.

13. Answers may vary somewhat but should contain the following points: Marriage is the lifelong union between one man and one woman. It includes a public declaration of commitment that also involves others (parents, the community, etc.). It is consummated in sexual union.

## *Day 4* • Mark 10:1–12

14. A certificate of divorce was to be provided to the divorced woman for her future protection.

15. Jesus guided the people back into Scripture and to God's original model for what marriage is.

16. The two legitimate grounds for divorce that are listed in the New Testament are sexual immorality (Matthew 19:9) and desertion (1 Corinthians 7:15).

17. Marriages are maintained and sustained through continual openness to the giving and receiving of forgiveness. Even in the Apostles' Creed, after we say that we "believe in the holy Christian Church" as a communion of saints, we immediately add "the forgiveness of sins."

## *Day 5* • Acts 17:16–18, 26–30

18. We are called on to treat all people fairly and charitably, regardless of their race, financial circumstances, or station in life. All people were intentionally created by God; therefore, we are to deal with everyone respectfully.

19. St. Paul stated that God made all the nations and peoples of the earth, and that all are descended from the first man, Adam. Therefore, strictly speaking, there are not multiple, different races of people, but only the one, united human race.

20. Paul had become a friend of a wealthy man, Philemon, who had a domestic problem. One of his household slaves had run away with some of the household possessions. The slave, Onesimus, was later converted to the Christian faith by Paul. In the letter, Paul is sending him back to his owner. But acting as an intercessor, paul asks Philemon to forgive Onesimus on the basis of their brotherhood in Christ.

21. Paul acknowledges that among people there are differences of color, gender, and vocation. These differences can seem, in various ways and at various times, to be extreme and even divisive. But Paul goes on to state that these differences do not divide Christians. Our unity with one another and with God through our faith in Jesus is of far greater significance than anything else.

22. Before followers of Christ were called Christians, they were called followers of the "Way" (Acts 9:2) because Jesus had said He is the way, the truth, and the life of blessedness in eternity. Early Christians told others that there is no other name (meaning "no other powerful person") who can save sinners. (Session 5 will deal with this in depth.)

# God's Invisible Creation

## Selected Passages

*Preparing for the Session*

### Central Focus

The Creator is so powerful and generous that He created various personal beings who do not require physical bodies or visibility to be complete. The Creator is also the loving Father who protects humanity from certain invisible persons in His creation that seek humanity's destruction. Their defeat by God is certain, and He wants humanity to use His weapons and thereby participate in that victory.

### Objectives

That participants, led by the Holy Spirit working through God's Word, will

1. appreciate the generosity of God in bringing an invisible creation into existence;

2. be realistic about the danger of the invisible demonic kingdom to God's people; and

3. actively join with God in using His weapons that defeat the agents of evil in creation.

### For the Small-Group Leader

*Small-Group Discussion Helps*

### *Day 1* • Psalm 103:20–21; Colossians 1:16

1. The word is "hosts." In some liturgies, they are referred to when God is praised as "Lord God of Sabaoth." *Sabaoth* is the Hebrew word for "hosts."

2. Angels are ministering "spirits," meaning that they do not require physical bodies or visibility in order to exist and to accomplish their activities.

3. Angels are aware of their self-identity; they refer to themselves by specific names. Second, they have emotions and thereby can interact with others, as Gabriel did with the aged priest Zechariah and with the young Virgin Mary.

4. Because they had a beginning as creatures, they were probably created sometime during creation week, before God "rested." Mostly likely, they were created before humans, because they are a part of God's support system for human survival (Psalm 91:11).

### *Day 2* • Psalm 91:1–12

5. We see that the angels are given control of the physical elements of the universe in all directions, from its winds to the power of the fire within the earth, which can be summoned at their command to fulfill God's will.

6. God used the angels to deliver the Ten Commandments to Moses on Mount Sinai.

7. Angels are present when the Church assembles in worship. Since they are God's "police" for all things being done decently and in order, disorderly worship offends them.

8. We must not be presumptuous to assume that our doing something contrary to God's will, or "testing" God's power to rescue us from some foolish action, means He will automatically send an angel to get us out of it. At times, God lets the wages of sin be collected in some earthly chastisement upon the sinner.

9. First, the angels pray for our survival when we are suffering for Christ's cause. Second, they escort us at our death, and on the Day of Final Judgment, to the wonderful presence of God and the new creation.

### *Day 3* • James 1:3, 12–18

10. The Genesis account is clear that God created everything "very good" (Genesis 1:31). This means that evil and sin did not exist at the very beginning and that God did not create them. Therefore, we should avoid the notion that God somehow is the creator of evil, or that it is the "dark" side of Him, and also the idea that the material world's essence is actually evil.

11. St. Paul stated that the existence of evil in the world that God controls is a "mystery" to human thinking.

12. The many names for the chief of the fallen angels include *Satan*, which means "the adversary" (Job 1:6; Acts 5:3), and the *devil*, which means "the slanderer" (Matthew 4:1).

13. In Revelation 12:9, Satan is referred to as "the deceiver of the whole world."

14. Satan often works in ways that appear attractive to self-centered people. He works in this manner so that he does not scare people away from the destruction he is deceptively working to bring upon them.

## *Day 4* • Matthew 4:1–11

15. Jesus tells us to pray, "Lead us not into temptation," so that we continually take into account our need to rely upon God to avoid the accusations and deceptions of the evil spirits.

16. Satan wants us to think that God is a self-centered deity who, whenever He can get away with it, withholds from us what we need. Satan is hinting that, to the Creator, we are merely a pile of clay to push around at whim.

17. Satan tempted Jesus because he knew the Son of God had come to give humanity a new beginning that would overcome the ravages wrought on the descendants of Adam and Eve for their disobedience and lack of trust in God while in Eden. Satan wanted to ruin this new beginning in the same way he ruined the original beginning.

18. Everything belongs to the Lord, and it is His people who will eventually inherit a brand-new creation (Matthew 5:5). Those who submit to the way of the Creator can see through the deceptions of false ways of exerting power. Jesus knew that from Deuteronomy 6:13, and He reminded Satan just who it is (God) that is in control, regardless of the circumstances.

19. God indeed provided for Jesus. He sent some of His good angels to minister to Jesus, probably giving Him nourishment. Likewise, trusting in the Lord, we know that God will provide for our needs in the manner and time that He knows to be best.

## *Day 5* • Ephesians 6:10–18

20. Satanic forces and enemies of God's people will try to prevent us from enjoying the victory. Therefore, as pilgrims walking toward the Promised Land, we must fight against those enemies who want to take away from us the victory under Christ, our King.

21. In both these passages, we read that we are given spiritually offensive and defensive weapons that are directly connected to God's power.

22. God will open to us a way out of very dangerous enemy territories where we may suddenly and unexpectedly find ourselves.

23. One door could be labeled "Prayer Chapel" (Matthew 26:41). When we come into God's presence, the satanic has to flee. A second door could be labeled "Armory" (Matthew 4:10). Behind it is Scripture, the sword the Holy Spirit forged for us. When we memorize God's Word, we can call upon it when thoughts or situations arise that are contrary to what God's will is for us. A third door of escape could be labeled "Assistants" (Hebrews 10:25). An old saying is "Burning coals set apart soon go out." The Christian community serves as God's cheerleaders for the team playing against the enemies. The Church gathers around God's Word and Sacraments, and it functions to exhort and encourage the soldiers of the cross.

24. Regardless of our circumstances, regardless of our situations, regardless of how impossible our troubles may seem, there is no reason for us to despair. We have a sure and certain promise from Christ that the gates of hell cannot destroy the Church of which He is cornerstone and the community of which He is the Head!

# God Is Still Creator

## Selected Passages

*Preparing for the Session*

### Central Focus

God remains in contact with every part of creation and with every person within it. Nothing happens without His control. God's control demonstrates His power and wisdom and also the faithfulness and care of a loving Father, despite the presence of evil and suffering now in creation, as He wisely moves it forward to a new creation. At the same time, humans are not robots under His power but have been given the ability to respond in faith to His promises and to be accountable to their Creator.

### Objectives

That participants, led by the Holy Spirit working through God's Word, will

1. acknowledge that God continues to direct, uphold, and enable all that He has created;

2. be confident that when they seek God's help in prayer, His answer will be for their welfare; and

3. focus on Jesus as God's deep love that redeems and moves the world toward a new creation.

### For the Small-Group Leader

*Small-Group Discussion Helps*

### *Day 1* • Acts 7:1–16

1. Answers may vary. Clearly seen in these passages is that God is in control of the great events of history—even the rising and falling of nations. He also creates life in the womb. His angels accompany believers through the valley of death into God's presence.

2. To ensure the survival of humankind, God blesses the earth with rain and fertile land for the growth of grain to support our physical lives. He also gives us His own righteousness in Christ, which leads us to stand in His holy presence.

3. Answers will vary. Perhaps what is seen as reluctance to change is really a fear that the change will make circumstances worse or not as comfortable as the present situation.

4. When Abraham passed from this life, he was welcomed into the eternal homeland, God's heavenly city. This is something that we, through faith in Christ, receive also. And so people with faith in the Savior recognize that they are merely pilgrims passing through the earthly landscape as aliens from another eternal land.

5. (a) Joseph didn't desire the spotlight to focus on himself, as if he were the prime actor on the stage of history. He recognized and honored the privilege of being God's instrument for good, even giving special names to his two Egyptian-born children that glorified God for His goodness to Joseph. Indeed, as Joseph acknowledged, God was again acting to save them (Genesis 45:5, 7), the descendants of Abraham and Jacob. The Messiah would be their descendant thousands of years in the future. (b) Joseph not only forgave his brothers but he also looked after their welfare and that of their families.

### *Day 2* • Luke 11:5–13

6. People who take the time to pray are those who recognize that they are not self-sufficient. By praying, they acknowledge that they need outside help, especially as they wrestle with the present.

7. (a) Christians may feel their sins make them unworthy to ask the holy God for anything. (b) Both passages show us that God is especially concerned about helping the needy, not only those with physical or material needs, but also, and more important, those with spiritual needs.

8. God wants us to persist in prayer so that we stay focused on Him and our real needs of life. Doing so will keep us from being out of focus, distracted, or anxious about who actually satisfies those needs.

9. Since sinful earthly fathers neither deceive their children nor give them anything harmful, "how much more" will our holy heavenly Father take care of our eternal well-being. This shows us that God our Father loves us infinitely and that we can always trust that He will provide for us.

10. God gives us the gift of the Holy Spirit that we may be sustained and encouraged in our prayer lives.

## *Day 3* • Luke 12:22–34

11. It is very easy for us, when struggling through the difficulties of life, to be consumed by the emotion of anxiety. This is the feeling of distress or fear about things that may happen to us in the future. It is the feeling that we are adrift or out of control and that we have no certainty that we will come to a good end.

12. This text teaches us the lesson that we are not really in control. But that does not mean that we are adrift and headed to a terrible end. For although we are not in control, we see here very clearly that God is always in control, even over the very little things of life. Jesus tells us that God blesses even the little birds and the flowers. That being the case, we can trust that He then blesses us, who are the very pinnacle of His creation, even more.

13. We are always to focus on the true and infinite riches of Jesus Christ. He is our bread of life that blesses us eternally and is far more valuable than perishable food and clothes that turn to rags in the present life. All else will pass away, but the gifts that we are given in Christ Jesus will remain with us and sustain and preserve us eternally.

14. While Peter kept his eyes on Jesus and trusted His promise, he was able to stay above the waves. But as soon as he focused on the waves and the apparent danger he was in, he began to sink. After pulling him out of the drink, Jesus chided Peter for exercising only "little" faith by his doubting. Likewise, we too are to trust the promises that Christ has made to us in the Bible, even when can't see how they could possibly hold true. When we are consumed by our doubts, fears, and anxious thoughts, then we are not fully enjoying that great gift of faith, for we are forgetting that God will in fact preserve us. It is at those times that a Christian's faith could be described as "little."

15. Christians value and hold dear God's continuing rule and governance (Scripture calls it "the Kingdom of God") in their life. This is truly of extreme value, for it means that it is God, and not sin, suffering, or death, who ultimately controls our destiny.

## *Day 4* • Exodus 9:34 and 10:1; Acts 2:22–23

16. Two truths, while appearing to be contradictory, both hold true. Each human being is responsible for his or her wrong relationship to God. At the same time, our response to God does not limit how He responds to us.

17. It is our conscience that forces us to acknowledge that all we do is being evaluated by another—God.

18. We see that God was working in Jesus' life to carry out a definite plan. We also see that it was God's permissive will that "allowed" Jesus' enemies to crucify Him. Nevertheless, God did not crucify Jesus; self-centered people did, and they—not God—are the guilty ones.

19. (a) As long as this present world stands, we will all face bodily death. But while they will have to pass through this, Christians, due to their redemption by Christ Jesus, will be spared eternal condemnation. (b) On the Last Day, God will resurrect all the dead and refashion the bodies of all believers into glorious, perfect bodies after the very glory of Jesus Himself.

20. God's control of the world should be encouraging to us at all times—especially during hard times. For we know that in the end God will see to it that all things—even the difficult and painful things—will turn out to our eternal benefit.

## *Day 5* • 1 Peter 4:12–16; 5:6–7

21. Jesus told His followers (and that includes us) to expect to face suffering at times. Because Christians are so different, others feel condemned by them and therefore retaliate against Christians and their different lifestyle.

22. It is one of the "secrets" of human existence that only the God who created us can understand.

23. Job trusted that God was good, powerful, and wise, and would one day give him blessings greater than his present suffering.

24. (a) That central symbol of the faith is the cross. For it was on the cross that Jesus' great act of self-sacrifice was performed to reconcile us forever with God. (b) Answers may vary. Emphasize that the crucifixion of Jesus appeared to be an utter defeat for the Son of God. His allowing Himself to be put on the cross appeared to be either weakness or foolishness. It was common sense that a wise and powerful God would not allow Himself to be taken and treated so cruelly. And yet in

what seemed to be a powerless Savior, God was actually bringing about the salvation of sinners in a way that so-called "wise" men never expected. Trusting in the "foolishness" of God (the crucifixion) is infinitely superior to trusting any great so-called wisdom we could devise on our own. We can always trust, believe, and rely on Christ, even when His ways go contrary to what we think is common sense.

25. First, Christians are called to take all their burdens and place them into God's hands. Second, they praise Him because they trust His love is with them to their eternal welfare.

# Son-Centered Creation

## Matthew 16:13–17; John 1:1–5; Colossians 1:15–21; John 5:1–29

*Preparing for the Session*

### Central Focus

*What* Jesus is and *who* Jesus is have been subjects of speculation and misrepresentation in the media. Is He just a man, though one of extraordinary religious sensitivity? What did He say about Himself? In this session, we will focus on Jesus Christ as the presence of God the Creator, come to earth to set free its inhabitants from theirbondage to sin so that Judgment Day will be the day of entrance into the full life of a blessed eternity for those who trust His claims.

### Objectives

That participants, led by the Holy Spirit working through God's Word, will

1. confront the life-changing implications of knowing Jesus' unique identity;

2. be confident that Jesus is the victorious presence of the eternal Creator; and

3. turn only to Christ in trust for the way to a blessed eternal life.

### For the Small-Group Leader

*Small-Group Discussion Helps*

### *Day 1* • Matthew 16:13–17

1. It is upon the rock of the confession of Jesus being the Christ, the Son of the living God, that Jesus has built His Church. We may trust in this throughout our life. It is in that belief that salvation is found. The fact that Jesus is the Christ is of extreme and even eternal significance for us and for others.

2. Jesus is the way. Who and what He is, is His message; in other words, Christianity is Christ. Unlike Moses and others, who spoke of a path and pointed people to it, Jesus said that He *is* the path to truth and to life in its fullest meaning.

3. There is no other name, meaning, or authority on earth that can bring a person into an eternity of blessedness other than Jesus.

4. If Jesus is not all that God is—indeed, the Son of God come down to us—then Christians have broken the First of the Ten Commandments. That First Commandment is foundational to all the rest. No one is to worship a mere creature or exalt himself to the position of God; we are merely of the earth. To do so is idolatry.

5. Apart from the spiritual regeneration of the Holy Spirit, who opens the spiritually blinded eyes of sinners, no one can recognize that Jesus is the Lord of Creation.

### *Day 2* • John 1:1–5

6. Consider the use of the word "with" In John 1:1: "In the beginning was the Word, and the Word was *with* God, and the Word was God." Here we have the Word being declared to *be* God and yet also to be *with* God; and yet there is only one God. Here in this verse is a revelation that, while there is one God, both the Father and the Son are God. Here we see two of the three persons of the Holy Trinity.

7. By seating people face-to-face, you affirm their equality. In the Greek text that is translated into English as saying "the Word was *with God,*" the word *with* has the connotation of "face-to-face." We could think of this as the Word being face-to-face with God and therefore equal to God.

8. In this verse, we find that the Word was involved in the creation of all things, and thus in the preservation and sustaining of the world and all that is in it. He is the source and preserver of all life.

9. The Bible lesson we are studying shows God's revelation of the promise and fulfillment of the coming of the Christ, who is the light of all people, unconquerable; He is the light that brings the life of salvation to those who trust in Him as their Savior and Lord

.

### *Day 3* • Colossians 1:15–21

10. We read to expect that during the last days, there will be many who will have no conviction or care about sound doctrine, but will have an interest only

in whatever tickles their itching ears. That description seems to apply very well to our present time. This may be one of the reasons why some people seek out so-called "nondenominational" community churches. These types of churches often have no doctrinal standard. Perhaps what these people are seeking is the license to choose which portions of the Bible they will believe and to have the freedom to discard the rest. Rather, we are called to hold to the whole counsel of God in the Scriptures and repent and change ourselves when we find ourselves living or believing contrary to it.

11. Answers will vary and will probably include suggestions such as television personalities, psychology, friends and family, astrology, and others.

12. We read that all truly valuable wisdom and knowledge is to be found in Jesus Christ.

13. Jesus knows what is important in creation because He made it, and He made it for Himself. It should be obvious then that we are to turn to Him to find our ultimate destiny.

14. The firstborn person is unique, with special rights and possessions. Logically, if one is in first place, no one else is in that position. Therefore, Jesus is to be given all the honor that belongs to God. To honor one who is not God, however, is idolatrous. Thus by calling Jesus the "firstborn," Scripture is demonstrating the divinity of Jesus.

## *Day 4* • John 5:1, 8–9, 17–20

15. Jesus took time from His busy schedule to go up to Jerusalem to attend a feast.

16. Jesus demonstrated this when He healed a cripple on the Sabbath, even though it brought down His enemies' criticism that he had broken the commandment to rest from work on the Sabbath. But His action was one more indication that He is God, who rightly knows how to interpret God's commandments.

17. People in the Gospel accounts spoke of God in the more general, pious way as *our* Father. Jesus, however, referred to God as *My* Father. This difference was an expression of His unique relationship with God, coming from Jesus' being the only-begotten Son of the Father and part of the eternal Holy Trinity.

## *Day 5* • John 5:21–29

18. There is much in our lives that weighs on us and burdens us and falls short of our expectations. It can be easy for us to feel that our lives have been wasted or that we haven't received everything we thought we had been promised from our jobs, other people, or what have you. It can be very easy to become disillusioned. As a contrast to that, in John 10, Jesus tells us He is the Good Shepherd who tends and cares for His sheep. In fact, He cares for them so much that rather than desert them to save Himself (as a hireling would), He willingly lays down His life so that they may have life and have it abundantly. Everything around us, like the hirelings, may fail us, but Christ the Good Shepherd will always be with us and uphold us. And that makes life truly worthwhile.

19. Jesus is the One who is coming to judge the living and the dead and who will bring the present creation to an end.

20. The only saving "good work" is the work of the Holy Spirit that creates the faith that unites us to Jesus' victory over sin.

# His Life: My Life

## Selected Passages

*Preparing for the Session*

### Central Focus

Non-Christian world religions stress that it is humans who must do something to placate an angry, hidden god. The devout will send their sons to die for the deity, sacrifice their virgins, or even tear out their own heart to make the god happy. The unique testimony of Christianity is that humans do not have to reach up to the deity or try to buy Him off with sacrifices. The wondrous Christian message is that God came down to be fully human among us, to experience all the negatives of our existence, and to die a most shameful death for us. God did this because of His love for creation and its crown, human beings. By entering fully into human life, and by living the will of God on earth as it is in heaven, the Son of God has obtained for us eternal blessings.

### Objectives

That participants, led by the Holy Spirit working through God's Word, will

1. rejoice that God's love for creation was proven in His full involvement in all the difficult stages of human life to sanctify it by voluntarily dying in humanity's place to bring it eternal benefits;

2. find comfort in their struggle with sin, knowing that Jesus remains forever their heavenly intercessor; and

3. walk through life with a vision of Christ's victory on their behalf that enables them to live like Him.

### For the Small-Group Leader

*Small-Group Discussion Helps*

### *Day 1* • John 1:14; Philippians 2:6–8; Hebrews 2:16–18

1. God established communication with humanity by becoming a part of it in its most fragile and vulnerable way: "The Word became flesh"!

2. Words are powerful and personal ways of making contact, expressing our thoughts, emotions, aspirations, and even love. When an infant begins to utter its first words, its parents almost immediately feel a deeper contact with the wetting, crying, and vulnerable little physical form under their care.

3. While God does not despise the material part of creation (such as the body of Mary), nevertheless, salvation is all through His initiative, His power. Humans have no power to save themselves. All that we can do, like Mary and Joseph and the Bethlehem angels, is to respond with awe and hymns of praise.

4. When God became fully human as the historical person Jesus Christ, He did not isolate Himself from the poverty of those who must work daily just to make a living. For He Himself worked and labored. He was tested by the misunderstanding of people all about Him, yet He never stopped trusting and doing the will of His heavenly Father, who acknowledged Him as His "beloved Son." When we bring our petitions to heaven's throne, Jesus, our advocate, understands them because He knows personally about what it means to have human needs.

5. (a) Trusting in God's beloved Son, we too are now beloved of the Christ's heavenly Father. Though our futures don't always seem bright, they really are; one day, when Christ returns to change the present universe, our honored positions at God's throne will be revealed to the entire universe! (b) We read in Romans 12:1–2 that our lives can be the launching pad that rockets us into the throne room of God as "living sacrifices." In other words, our lives are given over to God's service and safekeeping.

### *Day 2* • Romans 5:12–17

6. A cross was known throughout the ancient world as an instrument of a slow, torturous death. It was a symbol associated with death and defeat, not victory and life.

7. Jesus came to be the second and better "Adam." During His life on earth as a true human, He performed the will of God perfectly. This, of course, is what the First Adam failed to do while he was in Eden, and it got us all into trouble! At the same time, Jesus paid the pen-

alty fully for the first Adam's disobedience. By so doing, Jesus brought to all who are joined to Him through faith not eternal death but eternal life.

8. Satan wanted Jesus not to trust in the goodness and wisdom of saving the world in a way that didn't rely on self-glory and self-preservation. The first Adam of Eden grasped at glory through a fruit. But Jesus, the obedient Adam, continued to trust in God, even though it would lead Him to the cross.

9. We do tend to overlook the true and awful seriousness of our sinfulness. But God in holiness takes sin very seriously; God does not overlook sin. Instead, He loved us enough to take it personally. The Son of God experienced God's wrath to the absolute fullness amid the darkness of Calvary. There, the utter horror of our guilt before God was experienced by Jesus. Only because of His infinite holiness could He bear on Himself the sins of all humanity—and that includes ours. Such is God's amazing grace!

10. Jesus undid the curse of being expelled from Paradise due to sinfulness. In the Garden of Gethsemane, Jesus so trusted in the plan of His Father that He didn't avoid the suffering and the coming curse of hanging on a tree turned into a cross. By Jesus' obedience through suffering, He opened the door to anyone trusting Him as the path back into Paradise. In Jesus, "Paradise Lost" has been regained.

## *Day 3* • 1 Corinthians 15:42–49

11. We can remind them that Jesus' sealed tomb was open and empty three days after His corpse was put in it. We can also mention Jesus' many appearances in His glorious body after His resurrection. Here we have historical proof that death is not the end of life.

12. An important part of those sermons was that the once-crucified but now-resurrected Jesus Christ is living proof. He is heaven's receipt that our debt of sin has been fully paid so we can be freed from its prison. Additionally, those joined by faith to the living Christ will have a glorious life beyond their tombs.

13. Jesus had His disciples touch Him (Luke 24:38), and He even ate in their presence (Luke 24:41–43) to convince them that they were not imagining His presence among them and that they were not seeing a ghost.

14. Jesus no longer has to walk about from place to place or get into a boat to travel as He once did, but can suddenly appear in rooms with locked doors or appear in blinding light to be seen by whomever He wants to see Him (as with Saul on the way to Damascus). Jesus said that with all the power of heaven upon His resurrected body, He will be with His followers in all nations as they evangelize.

15. "Because I live you shall also live." Coffins and graves are only for corpses (Luke 24:5); they are unnecessary for the time when Jesus will give His followers glorious new bodies that will never perish.

## *Day 4* • Ephesians 4:8; 11–12

16. Answers will vary. Ascension may seem anticlimactic after hearing about the angels and the women rushing to an open tomb and all the other events connected with Easter worship services, such as grand music and plenty of flowers. Another reason may be that Ascension Day falls during the week (on a Thursday) rather than on Sunday, and so churchgoers forget to say to one another, "Let's go to church to celebrate!"

17. Jesus ascended into heaven in such a visible and dramatic way so that His disciples would know that the old ways of "seeing" Him walking and eating among them were now to be replaced by His invisible presence. He did say He would be within them throughout all the ages (Matthew 28:20). But they would soon learn that this would be through the Scriptures and also His hidden, but no less real, bodily presence among them during the partaking of the sacramental bread and wine.

18. In the Bible, clouds are often a sign of the mysterious presence of the triune God, who in essence is invisible. For example, a cloud hid the Father from the disciples with Jesus on the Mount of Transfiguration, so that all that was heard was God's voice out of the cloud.

19. God does not despise our bodily, physical nature. Through His own physical nature, He served others and died for our bodies' redemption and resurrection.

20. Wherever and whenever we bring His message, His Word, to others, He is present with His power to change people's lives.

## *Day 5* • Romans 8:34–39

21. "Sitting at the right hand" is a metaphor of Jesus being in the position of power to exercise all of heaven's

authority for the benefit of His followers, who are still part of a suffering community on earth.

22. Answers may vary but should include some of the following: Jesus is present in our lives from the womb to the tomb; Jesus is our stronghold in our spiritual battle with demonic spirits; nothing that is merely created—even time and space, which began with the creation of the universe—are governed by the Creator, whose love is limitless through Jesus Christ.

23. I have a personal representative, advocate, and intercessor in the throne room of the eternal Godhead.

24. Our realization of what truly is important becomes far more focused when we remember that Christ is ruling and governing the universe for our benefit. We don't take our value systems from nonbelievers, nor do we look to our greatest material possessions, as they eventually wear out or break. Our citizenship is in God's eternal kingdom, and that will never wear out.

25. Answers will vary. Certainly, we would want to include that Jesus is still very much alive, still powerful, still working on our behalf, and still desiring us to lift our eyes upward and square our shoulders and make our feet as light as if we were dancing at a wedding party.

# Heavenly Blessings through Earthly Elements

## John 2:1–11; Mark 4:35–41; 6:31–52; John 3:1–8

*Preparing for the Session*

### Central Focus

God in Christ is involved at times in amazingly direct ways in human life, using what He Himself created, in order to preserve, nurture, and bring abundant joy. Christians are called to activate their faith connection to the Christ of creation in order to face crises without fear but with confidence.

### Objectives

That participants, led by the Holy Spirit working through God's Word, will

1. find joy in how Jesus Christ uses His power for the benefit of the needy;

2. have confidence in the power of Christ to meet human need today; and

3. appreciate the Holy Spirit's use of special rites of water, bread, and wine as His vehicles of continual and unique divine blessing.

### For the Small-Group Leader

*Small-Group Discussion Helps*

### *Day 1* • John 2:1–11

1. Jesus was frequently criticized for socializing with sinners, but He said that as the spiritual physician He would go wherever the spiritually sick were.

2. The water had been set aside for the ritual purifying of the guests. This ritual was done to wash away any spiritual contamination that might have acquired by associating with a non-Jew or touching something the Old Testament Book of Leviticus said was to be avoided.

3. The coming era of the Messiah was associated with "sweet" (or new or rich) wine that will "gladden the heart" (Psalm 104:15) in the new land of restored Israel.

4. The disciples were feeling the "weight" of the Creator God present among them fully in the person of Jesus Christ.

5. By changing the water into wine, Jesus demonstrated that God intends to meet our needs, no matter how small (or large) they appear to us. He especially intends to bless our families, even from their very beginnings on our wedding days. This is evident from Jesus being present with the other guests to celebrate the wedding.

### *Day 2* • Mark 4:35–41

6. Answers will vary but may include troubles such as an unexpected financial loss or catastrophic illness.

7. (a) When the disciples looked to Jesus for help, they saw that He was sound asleep in the back of the boat. They assumed that He was ignoring their situation and that He didn't care about their welfare. Nothing could have been farther from the truth. (b) Jesus could rest comfortably because He knew that, as Creator, He was in control of the situation, no matter how threatening the scene was about Him.

8. Answers will vary, but obviously if you can still answer the question, you survived the ordeal.

9. Jesus was teaching both the disciples and us that we should trust in His power and compassion whenever we find ourselves facing a crisis.

10. Jesus is the presence of God the Creator among them and us. He is the ultimate ruler of all forces that seem to have the ability to destroy Jesus' community of believers—but they cannot!

### *Day 3* • Mark 6:31–44

11. By His relationship with these people, we see Jesus embodying God's "gut-felt" compassion for those who wander helpless because of their need of leadership and nurture.

12. He gave them the bread that they need for that day when He set the miraculous bread and fish before them as they reclined on the green grass.

13. Answers will vary.

14. Answers will vary but may include some of the following: Be organized in what you do. Use whatever you

have, even if it seems to be as meager as the small loaves and fishes offered to Jesus. Be confident that when you express a prayer of thanksgiving for whatever resources you have, God will multiply those resources to meet your needs.

15. From this we can infer that we have the responsibility as well as the power to do something that God can use and bless to alleviate someone's need (some examples: help with "meals on wheels," visit shut-ins, join a prayer group).

## *Day 4* • Mark 6:47–52

16. Answers may vary. Be sure to discuss that Jesus does expect us to work hard and to face life's difficulties. He calls on us to be realistic but not pessimistic about our lives. The road we walk with God in this life has plenty of difficulties—twists and turns, valleys, and high hills—to overcome.

17. We see clearly demonstrated here the divinity of Jesus Christ. Jesus shows Himself to be the God who walks through dangerous waters and brings people to a safe harbor.

18. We have strength in Jesus' invitation to stay focused on Him, call out to Him, and not be overwhelmed by what swirls about us.

19. Only Jesus is perfect. We are imperfect learners (disciples). Although we have a faith that could often be described as "little" (at those times when we fail to exercise it), nevertheless, Jesus remains with us in forgiveness and with the gift of the empowering Holy Spirit that revives us.

## *Day 5* • John 3:1–8

20. Our ears hear God's words of promise as water is applied and bread and wine consecrated for sacred use. We see the bread and wine, and we personally taste what we receive orally. Once again, in blessing us spiritually, God uses something from the material creation, which itself—as it has come from the hands of God—remains good.

21. The One who comes to us to bring us to faith in Jesus Christ and to keep and sustain us in that one true faith is the Holy Spirit. He brings us to that faith through the water with the Word in Holy Baptism. He sustains and preserves us through the Word we read and hear and through the bread and wine of the Lord's Supper.

22. In Baptism, we receive a spiritual rebirth and new status in the presence of God. From sin-ruled fleshy people, we're reborn as Spirit-led children of God.

23. We know Jesus was talking literally because of how covenants were always made among the ancient Israelites. A sacrifice would be made and blood would be spilled in the sealing of a covenant. Also, we can recall how God's people were saved during the first Passover. Blood from the sacrificial lamb was used so that the judgement of God would pass over them. Jesus is the new Lamb of God (John 1:29); God's people will never forget that, and they praise Him for it always (Revelation 5:6–14).

24. This is highlighted in the pronoun "I," which is God Himself. He absorbs His infinite wrath upon sin. Because the sin was against Him, the infinite One, only He could absorb the enormity of it and have human beings survive. Such is His limitless mercy and love. For God is not only the universe's Creator but also its Redeemer and eventual Restorer at the new creation.

25. The Lord's Supper is a foretaste of the great future feast of God's kingdom—the banquet of the eternal new creation, where all the resurrected believers will recline, eat, and be satisfied in the very presence of God and of the Lamb.

# Caring for Creation

## Selected Passages

*Preparing for the Session*

### Central Focus

Aware of their being given the privilege of being over creation as its trustees, Christians work hard to preserve the fruitfulness of the earth and all that is necessary for the continued existence of humanity on earth. This trusteeship includes Christians developing the energy of the mind with all its strength and becoming the disciplined spiritual athletes God intends them to be. The Christian's mission is to represent the caring Christ in all areas of life, home, work place, and government. Appreciative of the world's goods rightly obtained, Christians will use them to support creative methods for world evangelism.

### Objectives

That participants, led by the Holy Spirit working through God's Word, will

1. take responsibility for governing the earth's resources in a caring manner on God's behalf;

2. take control of their body and mind so as to reflect what God's redemption of them implies; and

3. adopt a lifestyle that influences culture for the better in all its aspects.

### For the Small-Group Leader

*Small-Group Discussion Helps*

### *Day 1* • Luke 10:36–37; 12:15; Proverbs 12:10; 14:31

1. Adam was given the assignment of being the caretaker and gardener of the environment of the Garden of Eden.

2. Unlike a dictator who cares only for himself, God's people care about the welfare of all those around them.

3. Answers will vary, but will probably include something like this: We've been adding to the destruction or pollution of many resources that are necessary to the survival of plants, animals, and humans, such as cutting down too many forests (the trees that are the lungs of the planet) or creating waste piles of substances that pollute the water.

4. Animals are not to be mistreated. We are to go to the aid of the poor and the needy.

5. Technology becomes a spiritual concern for us when it leads us to think that life's fullness is found in technological advances. We can easily assume that God and His instructions on life's meaning are unnecessary because technology can reach the heavens and bring the earth totally under human control. It is the assumption that "man is the measure of all things" rather than God.

### *Day 2* • Philippians 3:12–14; 4:13

6. One must be in control of one's inner thoughts. These are what our self-image is based on, and they form the basis of our self-esteem.

7. An "athletic" Christian realizes he or she must always be in training, be teachable, and be open to instructions from the "Coach." Such a Christian is not arrogant but realizes he or she is not self-sufficient (Romans 12:3; Galatians 6:3; 1 Corinthians 10:12). At the same time, the athletic Christian is confident in the rule book and the "Coach" (Psalm 40:17; 2 Corinthians 3:5) who calls the plays.

8. Trusting in Jesus, our past mistakes no longer condemn us. Christ has justified our existence. We can, therefore, stand tall and firm against the buffeting winds of self-doubt and other people's criticisms. And we are people who have confidence in our future (faith looking forward is referred to as "hope") because God's Word has told us of the great glory that awaits us there.

9. Christ has control over the thoughts, life, and actions of the "athletic" Christian. In response, the athlete keeps his focus on Christ and His promises. For Jesus has heaven's power and remains at our side, using it to enable us to walk with Him until the age of sin and suffering ends and the new creation begins. With such confidence of what awaits us, we daily push away all that is merely transitory, for those things are not worth the energy and devotion of members of Christ's eternal family.

10. Many days, especially those of frustration and aggravation, don't seem to fit into the pattern of our life as followers of Jesus Christ; we feel we are looking into a foggy mirror. Nevertheless, at the end of our walk of faith through this creation of decay and eventual passing away, we will see the face of our greatest love, our Lord Jesus Christ, and it will all be clear why we journeyed on earth toward Him.

## *Day 3* • Philippians 4:1, 5–8, 13

11. We are to guard our mind and thought processes and consider what occupies our minds the most. We can choose to dwell on what Christ has given us or we can wallow in what we lack. The choice is ours: to live in a victim mentality or to daily remember that we stand in victory through Christ.

12. We are not perfect, and yet we are when we are trusting in Christ's perfection. We Christians press on toward our eternal perfection as we daily wrestle with the sin condition that would slow us down, trusting always that we are as perfect in the eyes of God as Jesus is Himself.

13. We are not the followers of a dead rabbi, but of the living Lord. *Once* we were dead, powerless to deal with sin, but *now* we are enabled by the living Lord to daily fight against it. The more we focus on His victory on our behalf, the more His joy and peace guard our hearts and minds.

14. Jesus' own joy, which is centered in reliance upon the heavenly Father, takes over us. Carrying out the Father's will on earth, despite any temporary hardships, results in a God-pleasing life.

15. Christians do not get their directions from pop culture, but rather from sacred Scripture. And like a tree standing tall because it is nurtured by water, likewise Christians, who rely on the living water of the Holy Spirit, are enabled in their victory. We may always trust that He who is within us is stronger than he (i.e., Satan) who corrupts the culture around us.

## *Day 4* • 1 Peter 2:12–25; 3:1–7

16. Jesus has set the example of being among people wherever they are, both at times of celebration and at times of bodily and spiritual need. He calls us to live lives in imitation of His own holy example. Therefore, we see that we are to witness to the God who cares for the whole world through our lives of compassion and charity to others.

17. Christians are called to treat all people with respect. We are to attempt to take care of our own when they are in need. We are to be good citizens. And we are to be hard and conscientious workers for our wages.

18. Early Christian women demonstrated their faith in their lives through such things as being respectful to their husbands and by carefully managing the family finances by not buying extravagant things for themselves. In these ways, they were living witnesses of the humility of Christ.

19. If the husband is not open to feeling and listening to his wife's needs, then he has undermined his prayer life, which brings him consciously into God's presence. For in that way, the man has actually closed himself to seeing that the God who has mercy and compassion on the needs of sinners will react unfavorably to those who do not show godly compassion and mercy to others.

## *Day 5* • Luke 16:1–12

20. Answers may vary. But it may be that such people, some of whom claim church membership, have no awareness of how much it costs a congregation (lights, heat, paper, salary, etc.) to carry on its mission in society.

21. Moses asked for gold and other gifts to build a grand tabernacle to God. Jesus paid the yearly tax for the repair of the Jerusalem temple. Paul asked the various churches he visited to contribute to a relief fund for starving Jerusalem Christians.

22. In multiple parables, Jesus used the proper management of whatever one has been given as His way of making a spiritual application. Such is the case when He tells the parable of Luke 16:1–12 to His followers.

There is no assumption that the believer would not actively manage and take care of his possessions or finances; rather, we see just the opposite.

23. Jesus was calling on us to be shrewd in our present planning so that future needs are taken into account. For Christians, this means remembering that our present earthly actions go on into eternity (Luke 16:9b; Revelation 14:13), and that those actions are "good" when they reflect the love of God and especially when they lead others into that blessed eternity.

24. They may not realize that such actions reflect a shortsighted view of what it takes for the Church on earth to spread its message. Or perhaps the small monetary contributions are symptomatic of a serious spiritual illness; they believe that their stomach's growl is more important than protecting themselves from that growling lion Satan, who seeks their destruction and the world's (1 Peter 5:8).

25. Paul had been faithful to bringing the message of Jesus as Savior to all the places he visited. He had no regrets, and he did not look back. He was confident that he was continually moving forward into a better place. In all that he went through in his life of faith, Paul held to the promise that Christ, his hope, was waiting for him in the new creation!

# The New Creation

## Selected Passages

*Preparing for the Session*

### Central Focus

The present state of the universe, with the presence of sin and its negative impact, will end one day. Christians patiently wait for Christ to usher in the new universe, which will be without sin but will have, for all those who trust in Christ, the never-ending secure blessing of unobstructed fellowship with the triune God and with all God's faithful, resurrected people.

### Objectives

That participants, led by the Holy Spirit working through God's Word, will

1. be patient with God for still allowing sin and suffering in the world, even among His faithful people;

2. be confident that a future of unending joy and fellowship with God and all the faithful departed awaits them; and

3. be enabled for a lifestyle that reflects that of people who know that their future is with the triune God.

### For the Small-Group Leader

*Small-Group Discussion Helps*

### *Day 1* • Genesis 3:9, 15; Matthew 13:24–30, 36–43

1. Answers may vary. Probably, you would give serious thought to "zapping" them out of existence.

2. We can learn much from the Old Testament's testimony of God's relationship with His sinful people in the past. We see there that God is not quick to destroy; on the contrary, He is more than willing to let His love and mercy (which withholds immediate judgment) work their influence upon the sinner.

3. God desires us to proceed with patience toward unbelievers. He wants us to move slowly, getting all the facts to understand what is going on before we act. In so doing, we will exhibit a God-empowered self-control (Proverbs 14:29; 16:32).

4. In such a case, we are to be careful not to overlook the un-Christian behavior, but rather to slowly and persistently work to change the person's conduct. After time and persistent effort, if no change has occurred, that person must be excluded from the congregation.

5. Those in a right relationship with Christ the Creator will be heading toward a wonderful "harvest home," where they will partake of His glory. Unbelievers, on the other hand, like grapes that are crushed, will face eternal suffering under God's wrath.

### *Day 2* • 2 Peter 3:1–18

6. Whether we like it or not, or believe it or not, Jesus is going to make a sudden appearance in power and glory to end the present state of the universe. There are people who may scoff at this for any number of reasons. Perhaps they don't believe that Jesus will ever return, or that there will be a final judgment. Perhaps they don't recognize their own sinfulness. It is safe to say that if we don't see our sinfulness, then we are unlikely to see any need for a Savior. Other answers are also possible.

7. This was clearly seen in the great flood during the time of Noah.

8. God gives us the "big-picture" perspective that evil will be brought to an end in the final judgment. We have the promises that then the new creation will be ushered in for our eternal comfort. This sure and certain hope gives us the patience we need to bear our crosses, for we know that they are not permanent but that the time will come when they will be lifted from us forever.
9. Both Jesus and Paul knew (and we too are called to remember this) that God, in His own way and time, will justly revenge His suffering people. We do not need to add to our burdens by assuming the responsibility of paying people back for the offenses they have caused us. This is God's responsibility, and we can trust that He will fulfill it appropriately. This foregoing of any sort of vengeance is part of the patience and humility that we are called to in our lives of following Christ.

10. First, we are to remember that God does not work according to our time clock. Otherwise, we could become complacent and assume that the last days are far

off, forgetting that with the Son of God's appearance in first-century Palestine, the last days have begun. Therefore, we may expect our Lord's return at any time. And second, we are to be careful not to become easy prey of false teachers who claim to give specific details (not explicitly revealed in Scripture) about events preceding the world's end. God's Word is our only reliable source of information.

## *Day 3* • Matthew 25:31–46

11. Preceding Jesus' return will be the testimony from creation's earth, sun, and stars that Jesus is about to usher in a new creation. Jesus will then return. This second coming of our Lord will not be a secret but will be visible and obvious to everyone on earth. Every human being will see these things happening. And all will see our Lord's appearance when He resurrects the dead and judges all humanity. There will be no mystery about it, and no one will misunderstand who Jesus is or what He has come to do.

12. Everyone will face Christ, the "Lamb," their judge—rich and poor, powerful and slave. Even those who have died (and even those who have been cremated) will have their bodies restored and will stand before Christ and all the angels of heaven.

13. No, God does not predestine people to hell. As Ezekiel points out, God takes an oath on His own existence that He is on the side of eternal life, not eternal damnation. Those who are walking to destruction have chosen to live a life uncaring about supernatural things such as eternal salvation, God, Christ, and His message of divine rescue. Instead, of their own accord, they live in self-centered rebellion like the evil angels.

14. In and of themselves, the works that a person does are never good enough to counterbalance that person's sin condition. Only the unmerited love of God's heart (known as grace), embodied in Jesus Christ, is the source of forgiveness for transgressions and eternal blessedness.

15. A believer's good works are external evidence of the inner love, trust, and faith of Jesus Christ. These deeds were not performed in a calculating way so as to be deserving of reward from God. Rather, through the working of the Holy Spirit in us, our faith is embodied through our actions and conversation with others when we deal with them according to God's commands.

## *Day 4* • Revelation 21:1–22:5

16. One of the great and tremendous blessings of the new creation is that death has been conquered. We may always find comfort in the knowledge that when a loved one departs this life as a Christian, his or her soul has been taken to be with Christ in the very presence of God. And on the Last Day, the day of the resurrection of all flesh, the graves will open, and the bodies will rise again perfectly, without any impairment, injury, or illness, to stand body and soul together before God and the Lamb forever. Although they are gone from us now, they are not lost. And we may always look forward to a joyful reunion with them to come in the hereafter.

17. Answers may vary. However, the former things that will be no more include the sorrow that unexpected death brought to us or those we love. Moreover, all the things that once produced alienation and destruction (symbolized by the lion, or the wolf destroying the lamb) will never occur again. The peaceable kingdom of the Prince of Peace will everywhere be enjoyed.

18. In the new creation, nothing will take away the wholeness, joy, riches, and beauty (illustrated by the feasting and precious jewels). Through faith in Christ, our place has been "properly surveyed" within it.

19. One of the blessings we will finally behold is how everything that happened to us in life was used by God for our spiritual benefit as He carried out His plan for us. Previously, we knew this only through promise and faith. Our life is like a weaving between God and us. We are only permitted to see the underside and to trust that He knows what the great pattern shall be! In the new creation, we will finally see that great pattern of our lives. We will be permitted finally to see the measureless love in the face of the triune God, who created us, redeemed us, and restored us to the fullness of life evermore.

## *Day 5* • 1 Thessalonians 4:3–13

20. The purpose of light is to shine. Christians are reflections of Christ in the world and thereby impact the world for Him. Talk at times is cheap, but actions speak louder than words because actions take energy, passion, and commitment. Another verse of the poem said this: "All travelers can witness that the best of guides today are not the ones who tell them, but the ones who show the way."

21. The sex drive comes from God and is His instrument for the preservation of human life on earth. Since Satan is the agent of death, he wants those whose bodies are temples of the Holy Spirit to misuse their bodies and thereby dishonor God.

22. Paul here encourages adult children to support their widowed mothers. He also encourages the church to support widows who have no family to turn to for assistance. Even if they are not able to work at all, they may still honorably serve their families or the church through their prayers and supplications. However, Paul cautions Timothy not to support the younger widows who are able to provide for themselves. Doing so would not actually help them but would encourage sinful conduct, such as idleness or gossip. This being the result of sinful human nature, it holds true in the world as well in the church. People who are supported even though they are able to work are being encouraged to engage in slothfulness. As we read in First Timothy, it would be to their benefit if they were instead put to work according to their abilities.

23. Answers may vary; however, they will probably be that now we can shout, "This is the last time I will pay you, Death. It's now finished. You, Death, shall also die. Jesus, the Author of Life, my Savior, has conquered you. In Him, I conquer you. I am the victor!"

24. Answers may vary, but here is a sample: We are on a journey through a creation that will pass away. Along with the old creation, other things will pass away too; namely, all the negatives that prevent us from fully experiencing our dignity as baptized members of the family of God. We in Christ are realistic about the need to struggle with sin, death, and devil, but we are not pessimistic because Christ is Creator and Lord. We Christians are joyous in Christ, confident of the future, and full of praise as we move forward into the new creation.